Contemporary Studies in Literature

Eugene Ehrlich, *Columbia University*
Daniel Murphy, *City University of New York*
  Series Editors

Joseph Conrad

a collection of criticism edited by Frederick R. Karl

McGraw-Hill Book Company

New York • St. Louis • San Francisco • Auckland • Düsseldorf • Johannesburg
Kuala Lumpur • London • Mexico • Montreal • New Delhi • Panama • Paris
São Paulo • Singapore • Sydney • Tokyo • Toronto

123456789MUMU798765

Library of Congress Cataloging in Publication Data

Karl, Frederick Robert, 1927-   comp.
  Joseph Conrad: a collection of criticism.

  (McGraw-Hill paperbacks) (Contemporary studies in
literature)
  CONTENTS: Meyer, B. The secret sharers.—Karl, F. R.
Heart of darkness: introduction to the danse macabre.—
Van Ghent, D. Nostromo. [etc.]
    1. Conrad, Joseph, 1857–1924—Criticism and inter-
pretation.
PR6005.04Z758   823′.9′12   74-26572
ISBN 0-07-033321-1

Contents

Frederick R. Karl

Introduction

It was Conrad's belief that not only authorship but every other act of man can be performed skillfully; every act—whether the loading of a ship or the rigging of a shroud to the mast—if it is performed with love and care has in it potentialities for the craftsman. It is this love and care previously bestowed on sailing that Conrad transferred to writing. In a phrase from Boethius—". . . for this miracle or this wonder troubleth me gretly"—which stands at the head of the autobiographical *The Mirror of the Sea,* there is an evident equation of the miracle of the sea with the wonder of art. Still, Conrad's double devotion to the sea and to writing contained moments of doubt and soul-searching as well as moments of great love and confidence. As John Dozier Gordan wrote in his valuable study of the early Conrad:

> A slow growth from amateur to professional was characteristic of Conrad in both his careers. Until he was forced by misadventures to leave the Mediterranean, he was an amateur seaman. Until he was forced to accept his dependence on writing, he was an amateur writer. But once the necessary stimulus moved him, he had the power to achieve his highest aim, to become a master seaman and a master novelist.

When Stein in *Lord Jim* spoke about the necessity of immersing oneself in the destructive element of life, he was not only pointing the way for the redemption of modern common man but also for that of the modern artist. To plunge into life while endeavoring to interpret it, is the ordeal every serious artist must face, an ordeal that Conrad fully recognized in the Preface to *The Nigger of the "Narcissus."* It is not unusual that Conrad should have taken literature seriously and conformed to exacting standards, for his entire life had been a preparation for serious trial. His personality was earnest and his nature dogmatic; as his letters testify, he could not tolerate any nonsense in art or life. His serious standards were acquired as a youth; the broad range of his career reflects a man who faced up to reality and immersed himself thoroughly in life.

Conrad's father, Apollo Korzeniowski, was a scholar, an intellectual, a man whose strong principles became translated into revolutionary action, a patriotic idealist whose beliefs forced him, along with his wife and young child, from Poland into exile in Russia. Aside from his political activities, Apollo Korzeniowski had a lively interest in French and English literature, ably translating Victor Hugo, Alfred de Vigny, Shakespeare, and Dickens into Polish. Less than four years after Conrad's birth on December 3, 1857,[1] Apollo (in May 1861) came to Warsaw to start a literary journal, to be called the *Fortnightly Review.* Ostensibly, Apollo's activities in Warsaw were literary, but his real interests were political, specifically to increase resistance to Russian oppression, with the final aim of winning back Polish independence. He helped organize the secret National Committee, which met frequently in his own home. But even before the famous 1863 insurrection in Warsaw against Russian rule, he was arrested and condemned to exile. Conrad's mother, the former Evelina (or Ewa) Bobrowska, was a well-educated and sensitive woman who fully entered into her husband's interests and surely aided in his political activities. Co-accused of conspiracy, she was imprisoned, then with young Conrad followed Apollo into exile (on May 8, 1862) in Perm Province, not far from the Ural Mountains. Once in exile, Mme. Korzeniowski, frail, consumptive, and poverty-stricken, became steadily weaker and died less than three years later at the age of thirty-two.

Apollo himself in these years was a curious mixture of the romantic, practical revolutionary, landed nobleman, and poet. Many of the characteristics we find in the older Conrad, qualities both personal and political, can be discovered in his father. In many respects, Apollo was wholly admirable, a man ready to forgo personal glory for the greater good of an oppressed Poland. On the other hand, his activities against

---

[1]At Berdyczów or Berdichev in Podolia (the Ukraine), baptized Józef Teodor Konrad Korzeniowski (coat of arms Nałęcz). Józef, after his maternal grandfather; Teodor, after his paternal grandfather; Konrad, after two heroes in Adam Mickiewicz's poems, *Konrad Wallenstein* (1827) and *Dziady* (1832).

the Russian behemoth must have seemed foolhardy when Conrad looked back in retrospect at his checkered childhood. The dislocation, isolation, and discontinuity in his early life he, most certainly, attributed to his father's excessive zeal. Conrad's own political ambivalence—his predilection for anarchy and alienation coexisting with his desire for traditional values and social commitment—appears based on the divisions which began with Apollo's exile in 1862.

Without sufficient money to support himself or the young Joseph, Apollo was almost wholly dependent upon his less than sympathetic brother-in-law, Thaddeus Bobrowski. He retained, however, through all his misfortunes a love of literature. At this time he translated *The Two Gentlemen of Verona* and Victor Hugo's *Travailleurs de la Mer* into Polish. Removed from politics and immersed in literary work, yet broken in health and disappointed by his failures, Apollo died in Cracow in 1869, only eight years after he had arrived in Warsaw as an active partisan against the Czar. The funeral brought forth a huge display of patriotism on the part of those who remembered Apollo's political activities. The young Conrad, living in his father's strange world of broken careers, had occupied his lively imagination with books, which were almost his sole companions. Certainly a large part of Conrad's later emphasis on individual responsibility and his own strict self-control can be traced to his lonely, somewhat morbid childhood.

At twelve, Conrad was enrolled at St. Anne's Secondary School in Cracow, where he would have studied classics and German, but probably he never attended, another indication of the disruption in his early life. By this time, he was familiar with French, in which he became fluent in his later years. From 1870 to 1874, his studies were supervised by Adam Marek Pulman, a student at the University of Cracow. The discontinuity and irregularity of his schooling and family were beginning to tell on his health. He suffered from migraine headaches, and his excessive nervousness, according to Zdzisław Najder, may have indicated an epileptic condition. In his more mature years, Dr. Bernard Meyer tells us, Conrad suffered from an incurable disease of the joints. It is possible to speculate that his detestation of Dostoyevsky was partially based on the kinship he sensed with the Russian, extending even to their common physical ailment of epilepsy, although in Conrad the disease came to be manifest chiefly as nervous disorders or fits, without the classic symptoms.

It was during these years that Conrad confided to his uncle-guardian, Thaddeus Bobrowski, that he wanted to go to sea. All attempts to dissuade him were futile. No doubt his early love for the sea was a literary love, for in his father's personal library he had read a wide selection of sea and travel books. He became acquainted with the sea stories of James Fenimore Cooper, perhaps those of Marryat, as well as James Bruce's *Travels,* David Livingstone's journeys to South Africa, Sir Leopold McClintock's voyage to the Arctic, Hugo's *Travailleurs de la Mer* (which he knew in his father's proofs), and Mungo Park's *Travels in Africa.* Exile also enabled him to escape conscription into the Russian army. Certainly the most important reason for his decision was a need to escape confinement, a need, demonstrated in so many of his protagonists, to seek personal meanings, and a sea career offered one way. Conrad was early possessed by the desire to experience other countries. There is the now familiar and perhaps apocryphal story of his putting his finger on a blank space in a map of Africa and saying, "When I grow up I shall go *there.*" The *there* was the Belgian Congo, and his trip became the basis of "Heart of Darkness" and a major turning point in his life.

On October 14, 1874, two months before his seventeenth birthday, Conrad left for Marseilles and a sea career, armed with a few introductions and a small monthly allowance from his reluctant uncle. Shipping out from Marseilles, Conrad voyaged on French ships to the West Indies and to Central and South America; the frail factual basis of *Nostromo* was formed here, and it was on the *Saint-Antoine* heading for South America that he had his first experience with gun-running. Between voyages he found no difficulties in entering Marseilles café life. To his uncle's consternation, he spent his allowance liberally and soon went into debt. Most of his time was passed along the docks with fellow sailors, although in his more serious moments he attended performances of the operas of Rossini, Verdi, and Meyerbeer. Conrad also traveled in higher circles; in the salon of M. Delestang, the banker with whom he had been given credit, Conrad met several Royalists, and these meetings led to his smuggling activities on behalf of the Carlist cause, activities which he related in *The Arrow of Gold* (1919).[2] It was also here, his friend and biographer, G. Jean-Aubry, tells us, that he met a mysterious girl, the Rita de Lastaola of *The Arrow of Gold,* with whom he had a brief love affair. Reputedly the former mistress of Don Carlos himself, Rita was much sought after, particularly by a southern American gentleman, the Blunt of the same novel. Conrad, conceiving of himself as a romantic hero, as G. Jean-Aubry relates the story, fought a pistol duel with Blunt and was seriously wounded. A more recent biographer, Jocelyn Baines, argues persuasively, however, that Conrad's

[2]See also the section called "The *Tremolino*" in *The Mirror of the Sea.*

serious wound was not the result of a duel but of an attempted suicide because of gambling debts.[3] According to Baines, the duel was an invention of Conrad's and Thaddeus Bobrowski's to cover the suicide attempt, which was of course a mortal sin for a Catholic as well as a great embarrassment for his family. In any case, after his recovery, he saw no more of Rita and ended his Marseilles sojourn. Having spent four years in the French merchant service, four years in which he drifted from one berth to another with no idea of advancement, Conrad shipped out on the English steamer, the *Mavis,* on April 24, 1878, bound for Constantinople.

On the return of the *Mavis* to Lowestoft, Conrad first stepped on English soil, hardly understanding a word of the language. Little past his twentieth birthday, he decided, as he points out in *A Personal Record,* that if he was to be a seaman, he would be an English seaman and no other. It was, he said, "a matter of deliberate choice." After two years, in 1880, he passed his examination for third mate, and subsequently in 1883 and 1886, for mate and master. Two years later—and ten after entering the English merchant service—he had his first command, the *Otago,* from January, 1888, to March, 1889.

Just when Conrad started to write is not clear. In 1886, he began what is generally considered to be his first piece of fiction, a short story, "The Black Mate," unsuccessfully submitted for a prize competition in *Tit-Bits.* In the years 1887–1888, he perhaps kept a diary while at sea, just as he later kept a Congo diary. But when he began his first novel, *Almayer's Folly,* in 1889, he was still a seaman and by no means a dedicated writer. Conrad himself wrote in *A Personal Record:*

The conception of a planned book was entirely outside my mental range when I sat down to write; the ambition of being an author had never turned

[3]The first indication comes in the "Document" compiled by Conrad's maternal uncle, Tadeusz (Thaddeus) Bobrowski. The entry for February 1878 reads, in part: ". . . I got news from Mr. Fecht that you [Conrad] had shot yourself." Later, in a letter to Conrad (for 26 June/8 July 1878), Uncle Tadeusz reproaches his nephew: "You were idling for nearly a whole year—you fell into debt, you deliberately shot yourself. . . ." Even more conclusively, Tadeusz Bobrowski wrote to his friend Stefan Buszczyński (12/24 March 1879): ". . . wishing to improve his finances, [Conrad] tries his luck in Monte Carlo and loses the 800 fr. he had borrowed. Having managed his affairs so excellently he returns to Marseilles and one fine evening invites his friend the creditor to tea, and before his arrival attempts to take his life with a revolver. (Let this detail remain between us, as I have been telling everyone that he was wounded in a duel. From you I neither wish to nor should keep it a secret.) The bullet goes durch [through] and durch near his heart without damaging any vital organ." (The documents above are translated by Zdzisław Najder in his *Conrad's Polish Background* [London: Oxford University Press], 1964.)

up amongst these gracious imaginary existences one creates fondly for oneself at times in the stillness and immobility of a daydream.

It was soon after Conrad had begun *Almayer's Folly* that he was designated captain of a Congo steamer (in late 1889), an expedition (June 13–Dec. 1890) into Africa that became the source for "Heart of Darkness," and perhaps had as much effect on maturing his outlook as the trip to the Sakhalin Islands had on Chekov's. The Congo experience, Jean-Aubry and all future biographers have believed, turned Conrad from the sea to a literary career. Broken in health by malarial fever and a disease of the joints, but impressed by the desolation and base meaninglessness of what he had seen, he continued to write while recuperating. Moral, physical, and psychological breakdown, the focal point of his Congo adventure, was to become the major theme of his fiction.

When his health permitted, he returned to sea on the *Torrens* until July 26, 1893. It was as chief of the *Torrens* that Conrad first met John Galsworthy, and with this meeting their close friendship began. It was on the same ship that Conrad, on his last voyage, showed the manuscript of *Almayer's Folly* to a young Cantabrigian, W. H. Jacques, who encouraged him to finish the novel. When Conrad left the *Torrens*, he was never to go to sea again, although it was not for lack of trying.[4] *Almayer's Folly*, meanwhile, was finished and submitted to the publisher T. Fisher Unwin on July 4, 1894, where Edward Garnett, then a

---

[4]A record of Conrad's sea career follows:

Mont-Blanc, from Marseilles to West Indies, June 23, 1875–Dec. 25, 1875, as apprentice; *Saint-Antoine*, from Marseilles to South America, July 8, 1876–Feb. 15, 1877, as steward and junior officer; *Tremolino*, gunrunner from Marseilles to Spanish coast, March–Dec. 1877, Dominic Cervoni as captain; *Mavis*, from Marseilles to Sea of Azov, back to Lowestoft, England, April 24, 1878–June 18, 1878, as ordinary seaman; *Skimmer of the Sea*, from Lowestoft and Newcastle, round-trip, July 11, 1878–Sept. 23, 1878, as ordinary seaman; *Duke of Sutherland*, from London to Australia, Oct. 15, 1878–Oct. 19, 1879, as ordinary seaman; *Europa*, from London to Mediterranean ports, Dec. 12, 1879–Jan. 30, 1880, as ordinary seaman; *Loch Etive*, from London to Sydney, Australia, Nov. 24, 1880–April 24, 1881, as third mate; *Annie Frost*, Conrad injured, served for eight days as third mate, June 5–13, 1881; *Palestine*, from London to Far East, Sept. 21, 1881–March 15, 1883, as second mate; *Riversdale*, from London to Madras, India, Sept. 13, 1883–April 17, 1884, as second mate; *Narcissus*, from Bombay, India, to Dunkirk, June 3, 1884–Oct. 16, 1884, as second mate; *Tilkhurst*, from Hull to Singapore and Calcutta, April 27, 1885–June 17, 1886, as second mate; *Highland Forest*, from Amsterdam to Java, Feb. 1887–July 1, 1887, as first mate; *Vidar*, from Singapore to Borneo, Aug. 22, 1887–Jan. 5, 1888, as chief mate; *Otago*, from Bangkok to Sydney, Feb. 9, 1888–May 7, 1888, also for several months in Australian ports, as master; *Roi des Belges*, on Congo River, Aug. 4, 1890–Sept. 14, 1890, as first mate and master; *Torrens*, from London to Australia, several passages, Nov. 20, 1891–Oct. 17, 1893, as first mate; *Adowa*: Conrad signed on as second mate in Nov. 1893, but never sailed.

young publisher's reader, was greatly impressed with the manuscript. The novel was accepted, and Conrad, encouraged by Garnett, soon turned to writing another. While the evidence shows that Conrad was trying to obtain a command as late as September, 1898, he nevertheless continued to turn out nearly a volume a year for the next thirteen years. His entry into professional writing appears to have been a decision similar to the one he made when he chose a sea career: the need to seek his own valuation apart from the ties a man normally experiences.

Conrad's writing life extended for twenty-nine years, from 1895 until his death in 1924[5]; during this time he wrote thirty-one volumes of novels, short stories, essays, and plays, in addition to over 3,000 letters. Even with growing popularity, he remained, nevertheless, isolated from many of the principal writers and movements. He was an intellectual writer rather than an intellectual. For a major novelist, his circle of friends, although intelligent and devoted, was curiously limited to those of the old guard. His tastes tended to be conservative and safe. There were of course some exceptions—H. G. Wells and Henry James among them—but they were not in the circle in the same sense as Edward Garnett, R. B. Cunninghame Graham, John Galsworthy, W. H. Hudson, Hugh Clifford, or Edmund Gosse. Conrad seemed almost entirely unaware of Freud's work and the new advances in science, and entirely ignorant of older, established writers like Meredith and Hardy or modernists like Joyce, Lawrence, Virginia Woolf, and other experimenters in the novel whose careers paralleled his own. Among contemporary European authors of the first rank, he knew only the work of Gide and Proust.

Certain questions about Conrad's personal life, although interesting to the biographer, must perhaps always remain partially unanswered or open only to conjecture: for example, exactly why he began to write in English and not in French or Polish, why he first turned to the sea and then gave it up for writing, why he was antagonistic to his father's politics, and why, once famous, he remained almost completely detached from the chief currents of English intellectual life. At the beginning of Conrad's literary career, there was, perhaps, little more than force of will and an ability to draw upon all sources and all experiences.

---

[5]In the year of Conrad's death, another Pole, Wladyslaw Reymont, won the Nobel Prize for literature. Conrad was, however, offered a knighthood by Prime Minister Ramsay MacDonald, an honor which he declined for personal reasons. Najder argues that Conrad refused the knighthood because he was already a nobleman. I sense in his refusal a feeling of condescension toward MacDonald and a disdain for formal honors. He may even have recalled Matthew Arnold's lines in "Growing Old": "It is—last stage of all—/ When we are frozen up within, and quite / The phantom of ourselves, / To hear the world applaud the hollow ghost / Which blamed the living man."

His great power, like George Eliot's, lay in his ability to fashion strength of will into moral idea; and his life's work was devoted to "seeing" the moral idea from as many aspects as possible, until the idea became, as it were, the thing itself. Possibly, Conrad, already an exile in a strange country, perceived early that only in this area could he realize his talent, and any departure from it, he found, made him uneasy and unsure of himself.

Writing to Cunninghame Graham about Kipling, Conrad revealed just how frail his own hold on art was:

> Mr Kipling has the wisdom of the passing generations—and holds it in perfect sincerity. Some of his work is of impeccable form and because of that *little* thing he shall sojourn in Hell only a very short while. He squints with the rest of his excellent sort. It is a beautiful squint; it is an useful squint. And—after all—perhaps he sees around the corner? And suppose Truth is just around the corner like the elusive and useless loafer it is? I can't tell. No one can tell. It is impossible to know. It is impossible to know anything tho' it is possible to believe a thing or two. (Aug. 5, 1897, Dartmouth University Library.)

THE SELECTIONS

The essays that follow provide commentary on Conrad's major novels and stories and conclude with remarks on the state of Conrad criticism and scholarship at the present time, in 1974. "The Secret Sharers," from *Joseph Conrad: A Psychoanalytic Biography,* by Dr. Bernard Meyer, a psychiatrist, brings together three significant Conrad works—"Heart of Darkness," *Lord Jim,* and "The Secret Sharer"—and interrelates them with Conrad's collaboration with Ford Madox Hueffer (Ford), which began in 1898–1899. Since Dr. Meyer's method throughout his book is psychoanalytic, he is chiefly interested in seeing how patterns in Conrad's works compare with certain aspects of his life. For Meyer, biography and artistic achievement are inseparable. Meyer views Conrad's intense introspection during the period of his life from 1898, when he began *Lord Jim,* to 1909, when he wrote "The Secret Sharer," as being a result of the close relationship with Hueffer. Although the active collaboration of Conrad and Hueffer produced three works (*The Inheritors, Romance, The Nature of a Crime*), for Conrad, the relationship went far beyond that type of sharing: it enabled him to penetrate psychic levels deep within himself, to that world of divided selves that characterizes his fiction from *Lord Jim* through "The Secret Sharer."

In the essay on "Heart of Darkness," the editor of this collection addresses a similar theme, that of secret sharing between Marlow, the somewhat complacent narrator, and Kurtz, the predator and plunderer. Without minimizing sharing, the author of the essay views this long story as moving beyond the theme of sharing into areas that make the story paradigmatic of modern social and political life. Conrad's psychological insights in "Heart of Darkness," paralleling Freud's comments on dream interpretation, prepare us for the modern world, in which actual events are beyond credibility, beyond what the conscious mind can comprehend. "Heart of Darkness" turns reality into dream and dream into reality. Its images and scenes of breakdown and fragmentation, the author of the essay observes, make us confront not only our divided selves but also the great evil ordinary men are capable of committing.

Using Jungian archetypes, especially the silver as a treasure, as a "powerful *mana*," Dorothy Van Ghent in her essay on *Nostromo* focuses on the mine as a repository of the characters' moral values. Each major character must undergo an ordeal, and his survival depends on how he reacts both to the testing and to the fulfillment of his goal, which is attainment of the silver. The essential triad of questers, Van Ghent says, are Charles Gould, Nostromo himself, and Dr. Monygham. Gould lacks a particular kind of self-knowledge and is, therefore, an ironic figure of moral pretense. Nostromo, a man without any cultural base, is trapped by an economic determinism he cannot understand and, accordingly, achieves tragic stature in his quest for the silver. Only Dr. Monygham, the man who once broke under torture, comprehends both individual needs and the flow of history; and even he is a slave to his idealization of Emilia Gould. Flawed and destructive, the silver allows no one to escape its temptations.

Also working within a particular frame of reference to interpret the symbolism, Robert Wooster Stallman in "Time and *The Secret Agent*" sees the destruction of time as central to the novel. Conrad, he says, stresses circles, zeros, immobility, the zero meridian of Greenwich Observatory, and other comparable images of time and anti-time, so that temporal elements and anarchic forces (the irrational, the insignificant, the trivial) constantly war with each other. Stallman suggests that if Conrad has been able to undermine time itself, he has demonstrated the insufficiency of all theories, whether political, sociological, or psychological. All beliefs in this cynical, ironic novel are based on superstition and myth; all thought is muddling, all views nihilist. Stallman concludes that Conrad's irony is essential to his contention that modern life in a large city destroys all human values.

Rather than interpret the symbolism, Albert Guerard in his analysis of *Under Western Eyes* ("Two Versions of Anarchy") takes a somewhat different tack: he tries to pinpoint what makes the novel into tragedy and Razumov, its chief character, into a tragic hero. In many ways, Razumov follows the tragic path: A fatal decision drives him from his own plans into a wilderness of problems he cannot fully understand or control. One act leads to another until he is destroyed by an initial decision whose consequences he could not foresee. Guerard traces how Razumov is racked by inner guilt at the same time as, from without, he is threatened with death so that the potentially tragic quality of his character and of his mission is always before us. The content is perfectly suited to the ironic manner because irony itself is a way of concealing and revealing. Guerard emphasizes that the strength of the novel depends on Razumov—on his choices and disposition—and not on Conrad's view of the revolutionaries; this is a point that has been in dispute since Irving Howe stated that Conrad's attack on the revolutionaries seriously undermined the credibility of the novel.

R. W. B. Lewis, in "The Current of Conrad's *Victory*," does not consider that novel as part of Conrad's literary decline (see the final selection for that argument). Quite the contrary, he rightfully considers *Victory* one of Conrad's greatest achievements, belonging in the group that includes *Lord Jim*, "Heart of Darkness," *Nostromo, The Secret Agent,* and *Under Western Eyes.* After first noting the existential aspects of the novel, Lewis moves to a discussion of how Conrad used the materials of *Victory* to test the nature of fiction. Probing the structure of *Victory,* Lewis demonstrates that much of it depends on the doubling of characters and situations. Apparently, Conrad's observation of character and his vision of society necessitated pairings and contrasts. In *Victory,* Lewis examines Morrison-Lena, Lena-Ricardo, and Heyst-Jones, together with variations, all by way of showing Conrad's method: not to trace change in his characters but rather to make them increasingly visible, to make the reader *see*—the highest achievement of fictional art. Thus, Lewis notes continuity between Conrad's later work and his early statement in the Preface to *The Nigger of the "Narcissus"* that his aim was to "make you see."

Professor Hay, in "The Artist of the Whole Matter," attempts to deal with Conrad's often antithetical, paradoxical, and always ambiguous political ideas. Trying to strike a balance among several of his contrary positions, she shows us that he was a royalist who detested kings and leaders, a clearly political man who shunned politics, a Polish liberal who was suspicious of liberalism, an exile from Russian tyranny who feared and hated democracy but saw no alternative to it, a man who attacked socialism because in his experience it led to Caesarism. We can add that he was a practical thinker who dreamed of utopias and a writer who strove for perfection in an admittedly imperfect world. In England, he considered himself a Tory, and yet his fiction manifests a philosophical anarchism. A member of the Polish landowning gentry, he recognized the insufficiency of all political labels, and yet he felt nostalgia for the old world, the old ideas, the old order. Professor Hay's overview of Conrad's politics provides an excellent introduction to the sociopolitical undercurrents of his most significant works: "Heart of Darkness," *Nostromo, The Secret Agent, Under Western Eyes,* and *Victory.*

The final selection, John Palmer's " 'Achievement and Decline': A Bibliographical Note," not only provides a short survey of Conrad's fiction but also supplies a bird's-eye view of the current state of Conrad scholarship and criticism. Reviewing the line of development from Douglas Hewitt through Thomas Moser and Albert Guerard, Palmer offers alternatives to their contention that Conrad's literary quality declined precipitously in the last ten years of his life. The student who wishes to pursue some of Palmer's leads can find the material he mentions in the bibliography to this book.

As a final note, Conrad criticism and scholarship in the 1960s and 1970s appear to have reached a crucial stage. Critical studies have continued to appear, indeed to proliferate: Edward Said's *Joseph Conrad and the Fiction of Autobiography,* Norman Sherry's *Conrad's Eastern World* and *Conrad's Western World,* Claire Rosenfield's *Paradise of Snakes: An Archetypal Analysis of Conrad's Political Novels,* Avrom Fleishman's *Conrad's Politics: Community and Anarchy in the Fiction of Joseph Conrad,* Bernard Meyer's *Joseph Conrad: A Psychoanalytic Biography,* J. I. M. Stewart's *Joseph Conrad,* Paul Kirschner's *Conrad: The Psychologist as Artist,* Lawrence Graver's *Conrad's Short Fiction,* and Robert J. Andreach's *The Slain and Resurrected God: Conrad, Ford and the Christian Myth.* Of these, only the study by Meyer and, to some extent, the Sherry books break new ground. The others chiefly involve a rearrangement of known material or the creation of a position that required little more than a monograph. Most of these publications, clearly resulting from the proliferation of doctoral dissertations and the expansion of university presses in the 1960s, demonstrate no great urgency.

Except for psychoanalytic studies, already carried forward handily by Moser and Meyer, and Polish studies, now being taken up by

Zdzisław Najder, there are at present only two areas left for Conrad scholars and critics: textual studies of his manuscripts and typescripts—most of which are in American libraries—and close examination of unpublished letters. Textual studies of a comparative nature of manuscript, typescript, and published text have as yet been rudimentary. They should ultimately throw the emphasis back on Conrad's development as an artist, where the emphasis belongs. Similarly, the letters will reveal new aspects of Conrad's way of working and thinking and suggest new emphases.

Bernard Meyer

The Secret Sharers

Soon after he had made Conrad's acquaintance, Hueffer suggested to his new friend that he rent Pent Farm, near Aldington in Kent, lately vacated by the Hueffers who had moved to Surrey in order to be near the Garnetts. The Conrads accepted the proposal and a few weeks later moved into the house which was to be their home for the next nine years. Not long thereafter the Hueffers moved again and took a cottage at Aldington, which not only facilitated the literary collaboration of the two men, but established a proximity between them which was to endure for some time.

This change in his physical and human environment was accompanied by an unmistakable lift in Conrad's spirits. His letters, which so recently had been filled with melancholy complaints, now began to manifest a distinct note of hopefulness. Thus on the eve of moving to Pent Farm he wrote to H. G. Wells, "I am writing in a state of jubilation at the thought we are going to be nearer neighbors than I dared to hope a fortnight ago,"[1] and it was not long after this that from his new home he wrote the letter to Cunninghame Graham which heralded his seemingly sudden reconciliation to the life of a literary landlubber. Parallel with this change in mood there was a vigorous thrust of creative energy, for at Pent Farm Conrad seemingly struck a vein rich with the

[1]Jean-Aubry, *Life and Letters*, I, p. 249. Letter to H. G. Wells, Sept. 11, 1898.

"The Secret Sharers," in Bernard C. Meyer, Joseph Conrad: A Psychoanalytic Biography *(copyright © 1967 by Princeton University Press; Princeton Paperback, 1970), pp. 154–168 and footnotes on pp. 372–373. Reprinted by permission of Princeton University Press.*

gold of inspiration. Wearying of the literary dystocia occasioned by the vexing *The Rescue,* Conrad once again laid that troublesome story aside, and in December 1898 began to write "Heart of Darkness," which he finished with unaccustomed speed by the beginning of February 1899. It proved to be an achievement of singular importance.

On the surface the book is an account of Conrad's experience in the Congo. Indeed, in his Author's Note, written in 1917, he himself gave it credit for being little more than that: " 'Heart of Darkness' is experience pushed a little (and only very little) beyond the actual facts of the case for the perfectly legitimate, I believe, purpose of bringing it home to the minds and bosoms of the readers."[2] But to even the least perceptive reader this statement must seem unsatisfactory, for like many of his Author's Notes, often written long after the initial publication of the stories, it is clearly an evasion of the subtlety and depth of the work.

There had been a time, however, not long after the publication of the story, when Conrad himself agreed that it had a deeper meaning, for he charged himself with "the fault" of making the character Kurtz "too symbolic or rather symbolic at all."[3] Indeed, for Hewitt "Heart of Darkness" is a typical example of Conrad's ability to "make an appeal at two different levels: the natural and the symbolical."[4] Thus, when telling his audience of the effect upon him of the country and of Kurtz, Marlow says: "It was the farthest point of navigation and the culminating point of my experience,"[5] Conrad is alluding to a voyage "both into the impenetrable darkness of Africa and into the darkness of Marlow's thoughts. . . . We know that what Marlow finds in the heart of the African continent is a darkness which every man may be forced to meet within himself."[6] Clearly, "Heart of Darkness" is far more than "experience pushed a little beyond the actual facts." Unlike anything Conrad had written up to this point, the story is an introspective journey into the self, a daring attempt, in the narrator's words, "to find yourself . . . your own reality . . . what no other man can ever know. . . ."[7] Going up that river, says Marlow, the captain of the Congo River steamboat, "was like traveling back to the earliest beginnings of the world."[8]

[2]"Heart of Darkness" in *Youth and Two Other Stories,* Author's Note, p. xi.

[3]Jocelyn Baines, *Joseph Conrad,* N.Y.: McGraw-Hill, 1960, p. 227. Letter from Conrad to Elsie Hueffer, Dec. 3, 1902.

[4]Douglas Hewitt, *Conrad: A Reassessment,* Cambridge, England: Bowes & Bowes, 1952, p. 14.

[5]"Heart of Darkness" in *Youth and Two Other Stories,* p. 51.

[6]Hewitt, *op. cit.,* p. 26.

[7]"Heart of Darkness" in *Youth and Two Other Stories,* p. 85.

[8]*Ibid.,* p. 92.

At the farthermost point in his penetration of the river, Marlow discovers Kurtz, a European who had entered this wilderness "equipped with moral ideas of some sort," which he had memorialized in a scholarly 17-page report written for the "International Society for the Suppression of Savage Customs." In it he noted, among other lofty sentiments, that because of the almost godlike view that the savages took of the white man, "by the simple exercise of our will we can exert a power for good practically unbounded," etc. *[9] But in the course of his stay in the wilderness, a strange and ominous transformation had taken place in Mr. Kurtz's personality; like a snake shedding its skin, he had cast off all his fine European habits and ideals, revealing a creature whose condition of moral degradation and animal primitivism made him indistinguishable from the savages for whom he had once expressed such touching concern. Having reached this state he amended the sober 17-page report by scrawling across the bottom, "Exterminate all the brutes!" †

Mr. Kurtz, observes Marlow, "lacked restraint in the gratification of his various lusts . . . the wilderness had found him out early, and had taken on him a terrible vengeance for the fantastic invasion. I think it whispered to him things about himself which he did not know, things of which he had no conception till he took counsel with this great solitude—and the whisper proved irresistibly fascinating. It echoed loudly within him because he was hollow at the core."[12] Mr. Kurtz was under the spell, "the heavy mute spell of the wilderness—that seemed to draw him to its pitiless breast by the awakening of forgotten and brutal instincts, by the memory of gratified and monstrous passions. . . . This alone had driven him out to the edge of the forest, to the bush, towards the gleam of fires, the throb of drums, the drone of weird

---

*In his address before the Société de Géographique de Marseille on January 15, 1878, Henry M. Stanley spoke glowingly of the potential benefits that the white man might confer on the African natives, including their spiritual uplift: "When these people behold the white man stricken by illness, mortally wounded, and dying with the calm and peaceful resignation of a Christian, they wonder what is this Faith that sustains him, whence comes this confidence in a better future."[10] These remarks, widely quoted in the local press, were made on the occasion of Stanley's triumphal arrival in Marseilles, which took place while Conrad was living in that city.

†Aside from the suggestive allusions to Stanley, the character of Kurtz was apparently based on two other models: Georges Antoine Klein, a French agent of the Société Anonyme Belge pour le Commerce du Haut-Congo, and Major Edmund M. Bartellot, an Englishman noted for his "merciless ferocity" in the Congo.[11]

[9]*Ibid.*, p. 118.
[10]*Sémaphore de Marseille*, Jan. 16, 1878.
[11]Allen, *Sea Years*, pp. 277–281.
[12]"Heart of Darkness" in *Youth and Two Other Stories*, p. 131.

incantations; this alone had beguiled his unlawful soul beyond the bounds of permitted aspirations."[13]

These are hardly the thoughts of a man recording his recollections of "experience"; they are the thoughts of a reflective and troubled man, for the narrator of this tale (and of *Lord Jim*) is quite a different person from the Marlow of *Youth,* who interrupts his fond and wistful reminiscences with asides to his listeners such as, "Pass the bottle"; he is even further removed from his garrulous and misogynous namesake who tells the story of *Chance,* which Conrad finished in 1912. For the narrator of 1899 and 1900 is a thoughtful soul, skeptical, inquiring, and self-doubting—a perceptive and sensitive observer of the human condition.

Fascinated by what he sees in the wilderness, he is at the same time struck by the realization that the potential for a regression to primitive savagery to which Mr. Kurtz had succumbed resides within himself as well. What was shocking about the savages, he declares, was "the suspicion of their not being inhuman—the thought of your own remote kinship with this wild and passionate uproar. Ugly: yes, it was ugly enough; but if you were man enough you would admit to yourself that there was in you just the faintest trace of a response to the terrible frankness of that noise, a dim suspicion of there being a meaning in it which you—you so remote from the night of first ages—could comprehend. And why not? The mind of man is capable of anything," observes the astute narrator, "because everything is in it, all the past as well as all the future." *[14]

What, then, are the forces that spell the difference between the fate of Marlow and Kurtz? Why, despite his admitted "fascination of the abomination" did the former resist the temptations to which Kurtz had surrendered? "You wonder I didn't go ashore for a howl and a dance?" Marlow asks his listeners. "Well, no—I didn't. Fine sentiments, you say? Fine sentiments be hanged! I had no time. I had to mess about with white lead and strips of woolen blanket helping to put bandages on these leaky steam pipes."[16] Yet even this explanation does not appear to satisfy Marlow entirely, for he is aware that there are pressures exerted by elemental impulses that are kept in check not by the demands of

---

*Man is an evil animal," wrote Conrad to Cunninghame Graham at the moment he was completing this work. "Crime is a necessary condition of organized living. Society is basically criminal."[15]

[13]*Ibid.,* p. 144.

[14]*Ibid.,* p. 96.

[15]Jean-Aubry, *Life and Letters,* I, p. 269. Letter to R. B. Cunninghame Graham, Feb. 8, 1899.

[16]"Heart of Darkness" in *Youth and Two Other Stories,* p. 97.

practical necessity alone, but by the rules and conventions of organized society. "Here you all are," he tells his listeners in London, "each moored with two good addresses, like a hulk with two good anchors, a butcher round one corner, a policeman round another, excellent appetites, and temperature normal."[17] What happens, however, when civilized means of gratification are absent and external restraints are lacking? By way of example Marlow cites extreme and insatiable hunger: "No fear can stand up to hunger, no patience can wear it out, disgust simply does not exist where hunger is." Under such circumstances regression to savagery can become a powerful temptation: "Don't you know the devilry of lingering starvation, its exasperating torment, its black thoughts, its sombre and brooding ferocity? Well, I do. It takes a man all his inborn strength to fight hunger properly. It's really easier to face bereavement, dishonor, and the perdition of one's soul—than this kind of prolonged hunger."[18] In short, there are circumstances under which a man, even a good man, may be hard put to resist reverting to the beast which lies dormant within everyone. That which distinguishes Kurtz from Marlow, therefore, is not a difference in their basic primitive impulses, but in their ability or willingness to resist them. Stripped of these defenses against temptation, Kurtz and Marlow are one and the same—"secret sharers" of the same primitive core.

Indeed, in "Heart of Darkness," the first work completed after establishing himself in the former home of his new friend Hueffer, Conrad was embarking upon the first of what may be called "secret sharer" tales. A radical departure from most of what had gone before, in these stories Conrad employed the device of the "double" in his attempt to explore and discover those half-secrets hidden in the remote reaches of the mind. By recognizing his occult kinship with the monstrous Kurtz, Marlow too discovers "things about himself which he did not know . . . what no other man can ever know," and because he is dealing with perceptions hidden below the level of naked conscious awareness, this recognition contains an unreal and eerie quality, imbued with the strange elusiveness of dreaming. "It seems to me," he observes, "I am trying to tell you a dream—making a vain attempt, because no relation of a dream can convey the dream sensation, that commingling of absurdity, surprise, and bewilderment in a tremor of struggling revolt, that notion of being captured by the incredible which is of the very essence of dreams."[19]

[17]*Ibid.*, p. 114.
[18]*Ibid.*, p. 105.
[19]*Ibid.*, p. 82.

Clearly then, despite his later apologetic disclaimer, in "Heart of Darkness" Conrad had permitted himself to be "captured by the incredible," as he sought to open the doors guarding the slumbering chambers of the human mind. During the decade which was ushered in with the writing of this story he continued this inquiry, writing with poetic and imaginative daring, and often with an almost uncanny awareness, about that perhaps most fascinating of all subjects, man. In these years Conrad depicted him with all his inconsistencies, complexities, and unpredictabilities, caught in a hopeless web of twisted thought and tangled dream.

His earnest concern with psychic conflict revealed itself anew in *Lord Jim,* the novel to which he turned upon finishing "Heart of Darkness." * Like the latter, *Lord Jim* is a tale of "secret sharing," but it presents a far more painful and more searching depiction of mental conflict than is found in the earlier story. In "Heart of Darkness" the device of the secret sharer permits the "good" protagonist to maintain his integrity after he has succeeded in recognizing his potential identity with his evil double. Thus, while it is true that Marlow discovers that but for the grace of circumstance he might turn into a Kurtz, he is nonetheless able to emerge from the Congo with his ideals and his civilized character intact, albeit somewhat less sure of himself. In the case of Jim no such safe detachment is available, for when he encounters his "secret sharer" he is reminded not of any potential capacity for evil but of a real past in which he has exhibited a fatal flaw in his character.

The son of an English parson, Jim is a "good" boy, who, confronted by the supreme test of his moral fiber, fails. In the certain expectation that the leaky *Patna* will sink, he scuttles his seaman's code of conduct, and gripped by the instinct for self-preservation, he jumps overboard. Here Conrad's explanation for Jim's action discloses an astute awareness of the strength of obscure mental forces. Jim does not *decide* to jump as the other officers did. On the contrary when much later he tries to explain his action to the sympathetic Marlow, he speaks of it as if it had been perpetrated in a state of reduced consciousness, as in a hypnotic trance: "I had jumped . . . it seems."

" 'Looks like it,' I muttered," replies Marlow.

" 'I knew nothing about it till I looked up,' he explained hastily. And that's possible, too. . . . He didn't know. It had happened somehow."[21]

---

*Actually Conrad had begun, "Jim, A Sketch," toward the middle of 1898, but after writing a few thousand words he put it aside.[20]

[20]Baines, *op. cit.,* p. 212.

[21]*Lord Jim,* p. 111.

Psychologically these pages reveal Conrad in what may well be his most perceptive hour, for here he acknowledges not only that man may be torn by mental strife but that the outcome of such a struggle may stem from hidden sources of far greater magnitude than the forces of conscious resolve. Such a conflict is much more subtle and infinitely more frightening than is the picture of Razumov in *Under Western Eyes,* torn between conflicting conscious impulses: to safeguard Haldin's escape or to betray him to the police and thus save his own skin. When, on deliberately choosing the latter course, Razumov informs on Haldin, he does not say, "I turned him over to the police . . . it seems." Nor does Marlow ascribe the moral disintegration of Kurtz to forces lying beyond the rim of conscious control: since he was "hollow at the core," Kurtz consciously chose to answer the "mute spell of the wilderness" with a full-throated appetite for "forgotten and brutal instincts." There is no suggestion that Jim is hollow at the core. On the contrary, since he is a young man of high ideals and good character, his action is not a manifestation of a defect in his standards of conduct but a testimonial to the vast and undreamed of power of elemental instinct in times of crisis, instinct which resembles a reflex action in that, despite all contrary conscious intent, it asserts itself as the supreme dictator of behavior: "The mind of man is capable of anything."

Nor was the Conrad of *Lord Jim* any less perceptive in following Jim's slippery efforts to dissociate himself from his own action by ascribing it not to an impulse within himself but to forces without—a rationalization of behavior and action, incidentally, which Conrad was to espouse in his later novels. During his trial, for example, Jim tries to excuse his jump by blaming it on the officers calling to him from the lifeboat. "It was their doing as plainly as if they had reached up with a boat hook and pulled me over," he explains to Marlow, who observes, "It is my belief no man ever understands quite his own artful dodges to escape from the grim shadow of self-knowledge."[22] Nor does Jim himself, deep within his heart, really succeed in persuading himself of his innocence or accept his wishful efforts to project the origins of his shame-ridden conduct upon external agencies. For throughout the remainder of his life he embodies the image of a man seeking to undo his guilty deed. In this he never succeeds, and even when he has achieved the position of the beneficent overlord of the Malay settlement of Patusan, a new crisis arises which fans the ever-smoldering fires of his unextinguishable guilt: Patusan is suddenly invaded by Gentleman Brown and his piratical crew. Abandoning his habitual role of strong

[22]*Ibid.,* p. 80.

leader, Jim, instead of seizing Brown and his men and thus safeguarding the community, offers no resistance to the invaders and presents them with an opportunity to do their worst.

Thus, despite the fact that the seemingly redeemed Jim had achieved the status of a demigod over his people, the arrival of the evil Brown becomes the signal for him to betray them as he had once betrayed the Arabs on board the leaky *Patna*. But clearly, the motivations for these two betrayals are not the same: Jim's jump from the *Patna* was prompted by a wish to survive, but his failure to defend his people from Brown's treachery serves no such purpose. Indeed, it causes him to destroy all that he held dear, all that he had so laboriously created; it causes him to topple from his lordly eminence and to lose his own life. It would seem therefore that it is precisely to attain this end—his own destruction—that he commits the second betrayal, for in so doing he acknowledges and advertises his earlier crime. * What stimulates Jim's action, or better his inaction, is his discernment in the brigand Brown of a "secret sharer." Placing a finger unwittingly on a sensitive spot in Jim's defenses, Brown asks him, "Whether he himself—straight now—didn't understand that when it came to saving one's life in the dark, one didn't care who else went—three, thirty, three hundred people."[24] He asks Jim, about whose past he knows nothing, "Whether he had nothing fishy in his life to remember . . . there ran through the rough talk a vein of subtle reference to their common blood, an assumption of common experience; a sickening suggestion of common guilt, of secret knowledge that was like a bond of their minds, and of their hearts. . . . 'I made him wince,' boasted Brown. . . . 'He very soon left off coming the righteous over me. He just stood there with nothing to say, and looking as black as thunder —not at me—on the ground.' "[25] Brown's words thus rekindled Jim's sense of guilt and gave the lie to his assertion to Marlow at the Court of Inquiry about the *Patna* scandal that "there was not the thickness of a sheet of paper between the right and wrong of this affair."[26] Faced by the villainous Brown, Jim recognizes their underlying common identity just as Marlow had seen his "secret sharer" in Kurtz.

Lord Jim was completed in July 1900, and upon his return from a joint holiday in Belgium with the Hueffers, Conrad began a new story,

---

*His behavior recalls those misdeeds that are committed in order to "relieve" an already existing sense of guilt.[23]

[23]S. Freud, "Some Character Types Met With in Psychoanalytic Work: III. Criminals from a Sense of Guilt" (1916), *S.E.*, XIV, p. 332.

[24]*Lord Jim*, p. 386.

[25]*Ibid.*, p. 387.

[26]*Ibid.*, p. 130.

Typhoon, a sea tale again, but one which presents a sharp contrast to the recently completed *Lord Jim.* For *Typhoon* is the story of a ship's captain whose conduct under conditions of incalculable stress, unlike Jim's, epitomizes the best tradition of seamanship.

Like the *Patna,* the *Nan-Shan,* under Captain MacWhirr, is engaged in transporting a vast cargo of humanity—not 800 Arab pilgrims this time, but 200 Chinese coolies. Toward them Captain MacWhirr behaves precisely as Jim failed to do as first mate of the *Patna.* For MacWhirr not only guides his ship through terrible storms but concerns himself as well with the welfare of the anonymous coolies whom he brings safely to port.

The fact that Conrad was moved to write a straightforward tale of simple valor and steadfast adherence to purpose and principle only a few short weeks after finishing the story of the tormented Jim and his flagrant violation of the maritime code suggests that he was composing an antidote to the novel. It is as if in telling a story of quiet heroism and undeviating devotion to duty he was seeking to cleanse his mouth of the bad taste left there by Jim's neurotic suffering and erratic behavior. Moreover, in creating the character of Captain MacWhirr, an essentially simple man who is unencumbered by corrosive inner doubts or remorseless ruminations over what might have been, Conrad was providing himself with a respite, a breather, as it were, from the unlit and airless depths of the human soul into which he had recently descended.

Not surprisingly, Captain MacWhirr, for all his simple nobility, is hardly more than a caricature, a cliché. Although he has a wife—"a pretentious person with a scraggy neck and a disdainful manner,"[27]—she too is obviously a cliché; they have no personal relationship whatever. "The only secret of her life was her abject terror of the time when her husband would come home to stay for good." Their two children—also clichés—are "slightly acquainted with their father." Twelve times a year the captain writes home, begging to be "remembered to the children," and signing his letters unvaryingly, "your loving husband." And if the Captain's family is completely indifferent to him, the feeling is plainly mutual; Captain MacWhirr is first and last a simple sea captain, who "had sailed over the surface of the oceans as some men go skimming * over the years of existence to sink gently into a placid grave, ignorant of life to the last, without ever having been made to see all it may contain of perfidy, of violence, and of terror. There are on sea and land such men thus fortunate—or thus

---

*A favorite expression of Conrad's which he uses to denote an attitude of emotional detachment.

[27]*Typhoon,* p. 14.

disdained by destiny or by the sea."[28] "*Typhoon*," wrote Maugham, "is a tale of the sea, which he [Conrad] knew better than the land, and it is concerned with men, whom he knew better than women. These sailor chaps are a little simpler than most of us now think human beings really are."[29]

But if Conrad chose to tell the story of one of these "simpler chaps" as a way of coming up for air from the neurotic broodings of Jim, it was but a temporary relief. Hardly had he finished the heroic saga of Captain MacWhirr when he immersed himself in the passion and the mental torment of the one-time cannibal, Falk, and, shortly thereafter in the perplexing admixture of tenderness and cruelty of Amy Foster. Although lightened by the jointly written cloak and dagger yarn, *Romance* (1902), and interspersed with personal reminiscences in *The Mirror of the Sea* (1905) and *A Personal Record* (1909), Conrad's writing during this decade continued to reflect his imaginative and perceptive commitment to the complexities of the human mind. Upon the large canvas of *Nostromo* (1904), painted against a background of South American politics, commerce, and intrigue, Conrad drew the sensitive portraits of the neurotic and depressed Decoud, of Charles Gould, a man "haunted by a fixed idea," and of Emilia, his frustrated and neglected wife. His evident fascination with man's capacity for regression to jungle morality was revealed again in *The Secret Agent*, while the themes of betrayal, desertion, guilt, and atonement, so conspicuously presented in *Lord Jim*, appeared again in *Under Western Eyes* (1908–1910). Then as the "Hueffer decade" drew to a close, in late November and early December 1909, Conrad wrote "The Secret Sharer," a work which for some critics marks his last important literary creation.

"The Secret Sharer" presents the most explicit expression of the theme which Conrad had already developed in "Heart of Darkness" and in *Lord Jim*: the underlying kinship between all men—saint and sinner, Marlow and Kurtz, Jim and Gentleman Brown. The actual name of the story as well as some alternates suggested by Conrad—"The Second Self," "The Secret Self," and "The Other Self,"[30]—leave no room for doubting that this too is the story of a "double."

It concerns a young and inexperienced sea captain, who, taking the anchor watch one night, sees a man in the water clinging to a rope ladder lowered over the side of the ship. When the Captain brings the man on board he learns that the stranger, named Leggatt, has just

[28]*Ibid.*, p. 19.

[29]W. S. Maugham, *Tellers of Tales* (New York, Doubleday Doran, 1940), p. xxx.

[30]Baines, *op. cit.*, p. 356. Letter to Pinker, undated (Dec. 1909?).

escaped from a nearby ship, the *Sephora,* where shortly before in a storm at sea, he, the First Mate, had killed a disobedient member of the crew. Almost at once the Captain notices a "mysterious communication . . . already established between us two," while Leggatt observes that the Captain acts " 'as if you had expected me.' " The Captain says, " 'It was, in the night, as though I had been faced by my own reflection in the depths of a sombre and immense mirror.' "[31] During the following days the Captain hides the fugitive Leggatt (legate?) in his cabin. The Captain experiences a curious disturbance in his sense of identity—an alienation from himself. When he is temporarily separated from Leggatt it seems as if "part of me is absent."[32] His mind is affected, he believes, for he has become unsure of himself, neglecting to give orders which had always been second nature to him. Finally, after several days at sea, he selects a spot where Leggatt can safely disembark; the Captain brings his ship perilously close to the shore and his "double" secretly lowers himself into the water and quietly swims to the land, to become, like Jim, "a fugitive and a vagabond on the earth."[33]

There are other aspects of this story which evoke echoes of *Lord Jim.* Like Jim, Leggatt is an English parson's son, a subtle detail which imparts an accent of irony to their crimes. In another respect it is the Captain who resembles Jim—Jim in *Patusan,* seemingly secure in his isolation from the troubled world outside. On board his ship just prior to Leggatt's mysterious appearance, the Captain experiences a sense of satisfaction in his new task: "Suddenly I rejoiced in the great security of the sea as compared with the unrest of the land, in my choice of that untempted life presenting no disquieting problems, invested with an elementary moral beauty by the absolute straightforwardness of its appeal and by the singleness of its purpose."[34] For a moment one might have the impression that Captain MacWhirr is speaking, but suddenly this sweet tranquility is shattered by the irruption of Leggatt, just as Jim's idyll is broken by the sudden arrival of Gentleman Brown and his evil crew. And both the Captain and Jim, recognizing their kinship with these invading criminals, perceive that their dreamless sleep has become a nightmare, as they confront their evil other selves, their "own reflection in the depths of a sombre and immense mirror."

There is indeed a dreamlike quality to the nocturnal happenings in "The Secret Sharer," recalling Marlow's comments to his audience in

[31]"The Secret Sharer" in *'Twixt Land and Sea,* p. 101.
[32]*Ibid.,* p. 125.
[33]*Ibid.,* p. 142.
[34]*Ibid.,* p. 96.

"Heart of Darkness," for the language of "The Secret Sharer," the strangeness of its story, and the eerie atmosphere that pervades it conspire to recreate what Marlow calls "the dream sensation, that commingling of absurdity, surprise, and bewilderment in a tremor of revolt, that notion of being captured by the incredible."

What, above all, imparts to both of these stories their dreamlike texture is their amazingly intuitive intimacy with unconscious mental processes. The "notion of being captured by the incredible" expresses a flooding of the conscious mind by thoughts and feelings submerged or long forgotten which, seemingly without warning, pour forth and threaten to engulf rational thought and purposeful action. Faced by such sensations, man experiences uncertainty over his actual identity, anxiety over the nature and the power of his unknown impulses, and a deep concern over the cohesive strength of his mental organization. These are, in fact, the disturbing dream-like questions which obtrude themselves upon the Captain, jarring him rudely even while he is rejoicing securely in the quiet serenity of life at sea. "Who am I?" he seems to ask, when he confesses that "if all the truth must be told, I was somewhat of a stranger to myself."[35] "What am I?" he also demands to know, in remarking, "I wondered how far I should turn out faithful to that ideal of one's own personality every man sets up for himself secretly."[36] Was he the epitome of "immaculate command," like the Captain of the *Sephora,* or was he his "double," the killer Leggatt? And finally he is assailed by doubts concerning his sanity: "All unconscious alertness had abandoned me. I had to make an effort of will to recall myself back . . . to the conditions of the moment. . . . I had come creeping quietly as near insanity as any man who has not actually gone over the border." *[37]

That these terrifying doubts and questions were projections of the author's fears about himself seems certain. What is striking about them is that their expression in Conrad's writing was confined largely to a delimited phase of his literary career beginning with "Heart of Darkness," completed shortly after his first meeting with Hueffer in the fall of 1898, and ending with "The Secret Sharer," written just after overt signs of hostility to Hueffer began to appear in the summer of 1909. It cannot be without significance that these introspective journeys within the dark and shadowy passages of his secret self coincided so closely

---

*There is a prophetic irony in this line for it would not be many months after its writing that its author would actually go over that "border."

[35]*Ibid.,* p. 93.
[36]*Ibid.,* p. 94.
[37]*Ibid.,* p. 130.

with the period of his intimate friendship with Hueffer, whose moral influence was in itself apparently akin to that of a secret sharer, and who provided Conrad with a view of his own reflection "in the depths of a sombre and immense mirror." Just as two boys banded together exhibit far greater daring than each one alone—for the presence of an accomplice serves to dilute and divide the sense of guilt—so apparently did the spiritual union of these two inhibited men lend to Conrad, at least, a certain boldness in his willingness to search his inner self. He had rarely displayed this quality before he knew Hueffer and he was destined to show it with decreasing frequency following the dissolution of their relationship. And just as it is difficult to visualize Conrad shooting rats as a solitary pastime, although with Hueffer it became a source of joint amusement, so it is equally questionable whether Conrad alone, deprived of his friend's moral support, would have possessed the daring to explore man's "forgotten and brutal instincts" with the audacity manifested by him during the "Hueffer decade." What Marlow says at one point about Jim could have been said equally well by Hueffer about Conrad: "He was not speaking to me, he was only speaking before me, in a dispute with an invisible personality, an antagonistic and inseparable partner of his existence—another possessor of his soul. The issues were beyond the competency of a court inquiry: It was a subtle and momentous quarrel as to the true essence of life, and did not want a judge. He wanted an ally, a helper, an accomplice."[38]

"The artist descends within himself," wrote Conrad, "and in that lonely region of stress and strife, if he be deserving and fortunate, he finds the terms of his appeal."[39] Secure in the company of the "inseparable partner of his existence," Conrad could make that descent, emerging from time to time for breath and to reassure himself of the presence of his "ally" and "accomplice," and then descend once more.

And then, one day, his friend was gone and the alliance of the secret sharers was broken. Now Conrad resembled the Captain of "The Secret Sharer" when separated from Leggatt: part of him was absent, and no reflection of himself appeared in the depths of a sombre and immense mirror.

---

[38]*Lord Jim,* p. 93.
[39]*The Nigger of the Narcissus,* Preface, pp. xi–xii.

Frederick R. Karl

"Heart of Darkness":
Introduction to the Danse Macabre

From "Youth" to "Heart of Darkness" is indeed a step from youth to maturity as Conrad was aware. "Heart of Darkness," he said in the Author's Note, is "anything but the mood of wistful regret, of reminiscent tenderness," or the memory of romantic youth. To relate Conrad's development between the two stories to another author at another time, it is not unlike the passage from *Tom Sawyer* (1876) to *Huckleberry Finn* (1884) in Mark Twain's canon. The first is a study of a boy's growth which despite its preoccupation with the darker images of a youthful imagination is nevertheless a relatively light-hearted work. But its sequel, *Huckleberry Finn*, is a profound projection from a playful boy's world into an adult world of retributive and self-seeking evil. Dangers no longer lurk in the imagination but exist in the realities of the social world. From *Tom Sawyer* to *Huckleberry Finn*, there is implied a process of maturity which consists in facing up to the real world. Twain, like Conrad with "Youth" and "Heart of Darkness," moved from a youthful tone of "wistful regret" and "reminiscent tenderness" toward a larger and more mature view.

The comparison is not fortuitous. Behind *Huckleberry Finn* and "Heart of Darkness" there are a basis of similarity and a general kinship of idea, although the methods of each writer are frequently dissimilar. Central to both works is the passage along the rivers Mississippi and

Reprinted with the permission of Farrar, Straus & Giroux, Inc. from A Reader's Guide to Joseph Conrad *by Frederick R. Karl, copyright 1960, 1969 by Frederick R. Karl:* Modern Fiction Studies © *1968; by Purdue Research Foundation, West Lafayette, Indiana.*

Congo respectively, and the relationship between the river and the shore. Using the freedom of the river as a vast symbol, Twain opposed it to the deceit and treachery of the shore. Built on a series of contrasts, the structure of *Huckleberry Finn* is kept in balance by the very under-current that maintains the balance of the raft—the rhythm of the river itself—a rhythm that conveys the tempos of the novel. Conrad's Congo does not have the purifying qualities of the Mississippi, but it does lead up to and away from the stagnant jungle, the river Styx leading into an Inferno, and by comparison with the shore it is less tainted, less evil.

When Huck grows toward maturity and responsibility, an entire society is undergoing the rites of baptism, either gaining a sense of right conduct or suffering the loss of humanity. As a view of society, *Huckleberry Finn* is a very sobering picture, no less than "Heart of Darkness," whose dismal images of breakdown and expedience have so strongly engaged the modern mind. As studies in human degradation touched by the possibilities of regeneration, both works symbolize an era.

"Heart of Darkness" is possibly the greatest short novel in En-glish, one of the greatest in any language, and now a twentieth-century cultural fact. Like all great fiction, it involves the reader in dramatic, crucially difficult moral decisions which parallel those of the central characters, here Marlow and Kurtz. It asks troublesome questions, dis-turbs preconceptions, forces curious confrontations, and possibly changes us. With Kurtz, we sense the allure of great power. With Marlow, we edge toward an abyss and return different.

Conrad himself recognized that this novella penetrated to those areas of darkness, dream, indeed nightmare, with which he tried to define the substance of his world. "Heart of Darkness" helped solidify a vision that rarely wavered in Conrad's later work, and one we now accept as uniquely modern. Here he limned the images one usually encounters in dreams or in war, and here he found that discontinuous, inexplicable, existentially absurd experience which was to haunt his letters and his work.

Based on personal impressions, his own Congo journey, "Heart of Darkness" welled out. As he wrote apologetically and hesitatingly to Elsa Martindale (Mrs. Ford Madox Ford):

> What I distinctly admit is the fault of having made Kurtz too symbolic or rather symbolic at all. But the story being mainly a vehicle for conveying a batch of personal impressions I gave the rein to my mental laziness and took the line of least resistance. This is then the whole Apologia pro Vita Kurtzii—or rather for the tardiness of his vitality. (Unpublished letter, December 3, 1902.)

The novella, then, contains a vision so powerful that Conrad excuses himself for being unable (he thought) to control it. It was also, as Freud wrote of his own *Interpretation of Dreams,* an insight that falls to one but once in a lifetime. The reference to Freud and to *Dreams* is not fortuitous. It was of course chance that Freud and Conrad were contemporaries; but chance ends when we note the extraordinary parallelism of their achievements. Freud did his major work on dreams in the 1890's, the same time that Conrad was fermenting ideas about the Congo and personal and political expedience in a quicksand, nightmarish world. Freud's book, the culmination of his observations, appeared in 1900, only months after Conrad's "Heart of Darkness."

Chance is further reduced when we recognize that literature and a new style of psychological exploration have been first cousins for the last hundred years; that both Conrad and Freud were pioneers in stressing the irrational elements in man's behavior which resisted orthodox interpretation. Conrad's great contribution to political thought is his insight into the irrationality of politics, its nightmarish qualities which depend on the neurosis of a leader, in turn upon the collective neuroses of a people. Such an insight is timeless, but particularly appropriate for developments since 1900. For when has man tried so carefully to preserve life while also squandering it so carelessly? Conrad caught not only hypocrisy (an old-fashioned value), but the illogic of human behavior which tries to justify itself with precision, only to surrender to explosive inner needs. "Exterminate all the brutes," Kurtz scrawled at the bottom of his report. This is the politics of personal disintegration, uncontrollable personal needs, ultimately paranoia.

Confronting similar material, the scientist Freud was concerned with a logical analysis of seeming illogic—the apparent irrationality of dreams, on occasion of nightmares. Both he and Conrad penetrated into the darkness—when men sleep, or when their consciences sleep, when such men are free to pursue secret wishes, whether in dreams, like Freud's analysands, or in actuality, like Kurtz and his followers. The key word is darkness; the black of the jungle for Conrad is the dark of the sleeping consciousness for Freud.

In still another sense, Marlow, in his trip up the Congo, has suffered through a nightmare, an experience that sends him back a different man, now aware of depths in himself he cannot hide. The tale he narrates on the *Nellie* is one he is unable to suppress; a modern Ancient Mariner, he has discovered a new world and must relate his story to regain stability. The account is a form of analysis—for him and for Conrad. In a way, it provides a defense against Kurtz's vision.

Freud, too, returned from the world of dreams, an equally dark Congo—with an interpretation and a method, an attempt to convey order. His great discovery, like Conrad's, was surely that dreams, de-spite the various barriers the conscious mind erects, are wish-fulfillments of the hidden self. This sense of wish-fulfillment is evi-dently never far from Marlow—for the very qualities in Kurtz that horrify him are those he finds masked in himself. Kurtz's great will to power, Nietzschean and ruthless in its thrust, is also Marlow's. The latter, however, can hold back; his restraint, for Conrad, a mark of his Englishness. Marlow, however, only barely restrains himself, for, ir-resistibly, he is drawn toward Kurtz, readily accepting the latter's ruth-lessness as preferable to the bland hypocrisy of the station manager. Even Marlow is seduced—he, too, hides secret wishes and desires, his dreams curiously close to Kurtz's; and so are those of us all, Conrad suggests. Kurtz's savage career is every man's wish-fulfillment, al-though by dying he conveniently disappears before we all become his disciples.

The secret longing, the hidden desire, the hypocritical defense, the hate covered superficially by love, the artfully contrived lie—all of these are intertwined in dreams. In this sense, Marlow's experience is a nightmare for creator, narrator, and reader. The jungle, that thick ver-dant cover, disguises all, but most of all hides a man's real existence from himself.

As a connoisseur of dreams, Conrad is a ''dark'' writer in the sense Rembrandt was a dark painter, Milton a dark poet. They begrudged the light, husbanded it, squeezed it out in minute quantities, as if it were filtered from between densely packed trees in a jungle setting. So the light in Kurtz's heart barely appears, overwhelmed as it is by the dark-ness of his needs, the exigencies of his situation. Light and dark, in this vision, are polarized; their antagonism runs parallel to the struggle for life in nature itself, a Darwinian battle for growth, power, supremacy.

The yellowish, wispy light, indeed the white of the ivory, later of Kurtz's very bald skull, exists against the fragmented darkness of the jungle—the contrast of colors giving Conrad a vast symbol for moral, political, and social values, And yet such is the knottiness and am-biguity of his symbol that the result is blurred, filled artfully with the illusions and deceptions that Conrad makes us accept as the pathos of existence. Marlow, that pillar of truth and morality, does Kurtz's work at the end, lies to protect the lie of Kurtz's existence, ultimately lies to preserve his (Marlow's) own illusions. In an impure, dirty world, he desperately seeks a compromise—and finds it in the pretty illusions of naïve women. The very ground on which he stands softens and shifts. Marlow has indeed peered into the heart of darkness, his own as well as Kurtz's, and found as a reflection the very nihilism he fears. Needing to believe, he lies to maintain that belief.

To create order from such shards of nihilism, negativism, distortion, deception, savagery, and, ultimately, fear, Conrad offered a dubious restraint. Somehow, one must find it within. It is an individual matter, and evidently either one has it or one doesn't. It is not solely a European quality by any means, since Kurtz, that pan-European, lacks it, and the Congolese tribal natives have it. Restraint—a kind of muscular courage *not to do*—marks the difference between civilization and capitulation to savagery. Yet where does it come from? How does one obtain it? Does the lack of it always brutalize? Neither Marlow nor Conrad knows the answers. Such mysterious reckonings make it impossible for us to see Conrad as a meliorist. Society as constituted means little—only the responsible individual counts. Possibly one acquires restraint as the sum total of what he is. Yet decency, indeed the future of civilized society, hangs in the balance.

In this respect "Heart of Darkness" is one of our archetypal existential literary documents in which all is contingency. It fits the categories; it has the right psychology. The reader can, if he wishes, see the novella as a delineation of absurdity—that term applied to man's skew relationship with objects, with his milieu, inevitably with the universe. The images of the narrative, like images of a poem, intensify man's sense of alienation—right into the appearance of the pale, white-skulled, ailing, then dying Kurtz, an elongated image of wasted power and fruitless endeavor, the humanitarian now inhuman.

Possibly it is this sense of absurdity and discontinuity which so impresses Marlow that he returns a changed man. All his inner computers have broken down. This gnarled seaman is surely one of the keys to the story, and much has been written about him, including much nonsense. He is, at least here, Conrad's Everyman, Bunyan's Christian updated. What he suffers and experiences is analogous to what we as judicious democrats would feel. Conrad made Marlow sentient, somewhat intelligent, but, most of all, courageous—about himself, about life, about man's social responsibilities—yet at the same time sufficiently cynical; in brief, very much like Conrad himself. But the two are not congruent; among other things, Conrad possessed a literary intelligence that his narrator did not. He surrounds Marlow as well as enters him. But even if he is foremost a man of action, Marlow should not be taken too lightly. His intelligence is displayed in his moral sensibility. With a certain dogged charm, reminiscent of many American presidents and statesmen, he wishes to see the world based on English (or American) democracy. He accepts private enterprise—with personal restraints. He believes that imperialism must justify itself with good deeds. He expects all men to be fair and decent. Such are Marlow's preoccupations, and here Conrad demonstrated to good purpose the contradictions and rifts between modern belief and modern practice. And here also is the source of Conrad's irony—a quality that gives him considerable advantage over Marlow.

Since he is a man of order and moral courage, Marlow expects similar restraints to prevail elsewhere. As a captain he of course knows that such qualities are essential to preserve life at sea. Carrying them over into civilian life, they become for him psychological expectations. Marlow acquiesces to the world's work as basically just and fundamentally good, even necessary, provided it is done by enlightened men. Like Conrad, he accepts the status quo, but one maintained, he trusts, by just men. For both this is the sole basis of the human contract—one does things in an enlightened manner and develops his moral sensibilities. This is a solid nineteenth-century philosophy, although for us somewhat naïve. Marlow rarely questions whether particular work is necessary; for example, he never asks whether white men should be in the Congo—for whatever reason. Rather, he assumes they should be —since they are—but they must come as friends, as helpers, and bring enlightenment. Even while they rape, they must be benevolent. He sees them as solid, progressive Englishmen, who helped to develop countries the better to plunder them, nineteenth-century "ugly Americans."

Marlow's great revelation comes when he sees that the world is not arranged this way—and here the Congo is a microcosm of the great world in which those who can, plunder those who cannot. Marlow's awareness of evil comes when he notes that many men, and those the most willful, do not share his belief in an orderly, enlightened society. Theirs is one of chaos, anarchy, "unspeakable rites." They approve human sacrifice, and they eat their victims. This is Conrad's existential wedge, so to speak. A law-abiding, morally sensitive man enters an avaricious, predatory, almost psychopathic world. For the moment he sees that civilization brings dubious rewards. He learns the harsh vocabulary of reality. He matures. The nineteenth century becomes the twentieth.

The long river that informs this world is described, like the Styx, in treacherous, serpentine terms—"deadly—like a snake," "resembling an immense snake uncoiled." The river is essentially a woman: dangerous, dark, mysterious, concealed, with the jungle also feminine, personified by Kurtz's savage mistress. Marlow is overwhelmed; his ideal of womanhood is clearly the girl back in Brussels, or his aunt—the brainwashed public—that naïve woman who believes "the labourer is worthy of his hire." Such womanly illusions Marlow wishes to preserve. But his experience includes a treacherous, feminine river, an equally perfidious jungle that conceals its terrors, and, finally, a savage mistress—in all, an unspeakable sexual experience. Though the reticent, chivalrous Marlow never speaks directly of sex, it lies heavily on the story, in every aspect of nature—in *his* fears, in *its* demands. As much as Marlow fears the attraction of power, he shies away from the temptation of orgiastic, uncontrollable sex. He retreats into neutral shock.

Clearly, every facet of Marlow's experience in the Congo, including his preliminary interview in the Brussels office, contains elements of the absurd—that is, elements that become a wedge between man's seeming rationality and a world suddenly irrational and out of focus. The question is not Hamlet's, but how one should live. If absurdity is acknowledged, what are a man's guidelines? Does one concern oneself with morality or conscience? And even so, what sustains a man when tempted by the devil within, by corruption without? What is restraint if it isolates?

In a letter to Cunninghame Graham, written while "Heart of Darkness" was welling up, Conrad revealed his most personal fears: that in a world of ever-shifting illusions, what ultimately, if anything, does matter? Who finally, if anyone, does care?

> In a dispassionate view the ardour for reform, improvement for virtue, for knowledge, and even for beauty is only a vain sticking up for appearances as though one were anxious about the cut of one's clothes in a community of blind men. Life knows us not and we do not know life—we don't know even our own thoughts. Half the words we use have no meaning whatever and of the other half each man understands each word after the fashion of his own folly and conceit. Faith is a myth and beliefs shift like mists on the shore; thoughts vanish; words, once pronounced, die; and the memory of yesterday is as shadowy as the hope of to-morrow—only the string of my platitudes seems to have no end. As our [Polish] peasants say: "Pray, brother, forgive me for the love of God." And we don't know what forgiveness is, nor what is love, nor where God is, Assez. (January 14, 1898, Dartmouth University Library)

"Heart of Darkness," then, is concerned with moral issues in their most troubling sense: not only as philosophical imperatives, but practically, as they work out in human behavior. In a mechanical universe—"evolved out of a chaos of scraps of iron"—what is flesh? The profusion of metallic and mechanical images indicates that resistant objects have superseded softness, flexibility, humanity itself; that, clearly, one must become an object, tough and durable, in order to survive.

Once again to Cunninghame Graham (Feb. 8, 1899, Yale U. Library), Conrad stressed apropos of "Heart of Darkness" that he didn't start "with an abstract notion" but with "definite images." Such images abound: from the ludicrous French gunboat to its shells lobbed indiscriminately into the bush, then the metal of nuts and bolts and decaying, overturned equipment, the rusted steamboat settled in the mud, even the polished, unnatural accountant at the station, with the land itself silhouetted by withered natives, shades of themselves, victims of an imperialist Inferno, now dried, inhuman, lacking flesh or spirit, too soft for modern life. And dominating all, the smoothly metallic, white, luxurious ivory.

The sense of human waste that pervades the story is best unfolded in the ivory itself. It is an object for the rich—in decorations, for piano keys, for bibelots—hardly necessary for physical or mental survival. In a way, it is like art, a social luxury, and it is for art that the Congo is plundered and untold numbers slaughtered brutally, or casually. This view of ivory as art was surely part of Conrad's conception; a utilitarian object would have had its own raison d'être. A relatively useless item or one selective in its market only points up the horror; surely this, too, is part of Kurtz's vision. Possibly Kurtz's artistic propensities (he paints, he collects human heads, he seeks ivory) make him so contemptuous of individual lives; for art and life have always warred. In the name of art (pyramids, churches, tombs, monuments, palaces), how many have died, gone without, worked as slaves? Traditionally, beauty for the few is gained with blood of the many.

Where art rules, artifacts are a form of power. The art object takes on magical significance, becoming a kind of totem, the fairy-tale golden egg. Knowing this, Kurtz gains his power, indeed his identity and being, from the ivory he covets. In a world of art, the most greedy collector is often supreme; matter, not manner, counts. One source of Kurtz's fascination for Marlow is the former's will to power, Nietzschean, superhuman, and brutal. Kurtz has risen above the masses—of natives, station managers, even of directors back in Brussels. He must continue to assert himself, a megalomaniac in search of further power. Marlow has never met anyone like him, this Kurtz who represents all of Europe. The insulated Englishman now faces east, toward the continent. "I took great care to give a cosmopolitan origin to Kurtz," Conrad noted in a letter to K. Waliszewski (Dec. 16, 1903, *Lettres françaises*). "All Europe contributed to the making of Kurtz," we read.

He is indeed Europe, searching for power, maneuvering for advantage; and he finds it in the colonial adventure of ivory. No wonder, then, that his hunger for acquisition is so overwhelming. Having gratified forbidden desires, he is free of civilized taboos. In the Congo, where the white man—the civilized Belgian—ruled, he could do anything. His only prescription: produce results, send back ivory. Indeed, his very will to power, his confident brutality made him appear a kind of god—to the natives and other agents who feared him, to the Russian sailor who believed in him.

The ultimate corruption is that Kurtz can go his way without restraint. All human barriers are down. Only power counts—no matter whether political or economic. In the jungle, as in enterprise, only the strong survive, and Kurtz obviously is one of the strong. He brings European power—all of Europe—into the jungle; his weapons encompass 2,000 years of Western civilization. And the consequence: corruption of self and death to "inferiors" on a monumental scale.

When a journalist informs Marlow that Kurtz would have been a "splendid leader of an extreme party," Marlow understandably asks, "What party?" "Any party," his visitor answers. "He was an—an extremist." With that, Conrad presents his grandest insight into the politics of our time—superficially totalitarian, but extending also to democratic powers. The absence of social morality, the desire to rise at everyone's expense, the manipulation of whole peoples for purely selfish ends, the obsession with image and consensus, and personal power, the absence of meaningful beliefs, the drive for advancement and aggrandizement without larger considerations, the career built on manipulation and strategies, not ideas—all of these have become the expected burden of the ruled in our century. The rapist here is Belgian, later German, Russian, American—with the scale varying. The great symbol of our times is the chameleon—one can be all things to all men. This, we are reminded, in a society proud of having turned the corner into democracy, decency, and dignity. The best lack all conviction, as Yeats was later to write, while the worst—they act.

In this conception of Kurtz, Conrad's powers as an artistic thinker were at their strongest. In reading Conrad it is often necessary to discriminate between pure thought and thought embodied in a work of art. As a political and social theorist, he was antagonistic to modern developments, deeply conservative in the sense that he suspected or mocked new departures or experiments. As an artistic thinker, however, he was at once caustic, subtle, broad. His conception of Kurtz, slim on the surface, broadening beneath, is a Cassandra's view of European progress, a view both realistic and ironic.

Conrad was concerned with the rape of a people. The Congo had been, since 1875, the private preserve of Leopold II of Belgium, a medieval kingdom for personal use, organized under the deceptive title of the International Association for the Civilization of Central Africa. Demographists estimate that hundreds of thousands, possibly millions, of Congolese died in slavery or through brutality; a beginner's course in Nazism. Kurtz, or his type of exploiter, was the rule, not the exception. Kurtz himself was based roughly and loosely on one Georges-Antoine Klein (Klein = small, Kurtz = short), whom Conrad had taken aboard his steamer during *his* Congo days. Conrad's journey, as he relates in his Congo diary, was real, Kurtz and his type prevailed, the land and the natives existed, the facts are undisputed. Even if Conrad used symbols to excess, as he feared, each symbol is solidly grounded in fact. Here is white against black, entrenched against primitive, have against have-not, machine against spear, civilization against tribe.

If Conrad's novella is to have artistic as well as political significance, it must make broad reference to human motivation and behavior. One evident part of the application comes with Kurtz's double shriek of "The horror! The horror!" The cry is far richer and more ambiguous than most readers make it. We must remember that Marlow is reporting, and Marlow has a particular view and need of Kurtz. As Marlow understands the scream, it represents a moral victory; that is, on the threshold of death, Kurtz has reviewed his life with all its horror and in some dying part of him has repented. Marlow hears the words as a victory of moral sensibility over a life of brutality and prostituted ideals. This "Christian" reading of the words is, of course, what Marlow himself wishes to hear; he is a moral man, and he believes, with this kind of bourgeois religiosity, that all men ultimately repent when confronted by the great unknown. Kurtz's cry, in this interpretation, fits in with what Marlow wants to know of human nature.

We are not all Marlows, however, and we should not be seduced into agreeing with him, even if he is partially right. More ambiguously and ironically, Kurtz's cry might be a shriek of despair that after having accomplished so little he must now perish. His horror is the anguish of one who dies with his work incomplete. In this view, Kurtz does not repent; rather, he bewails a fate which frustrates his plans. Indeed, at the very moment of death, he challenges life and death and tries to make his baffled will prevail. Like Milton's Satan, he prefers hell to compromise.

Conrad's grasp of moral issues remained unresolved; he always harked back to the individual devil in each man— perhaps as part of his Catholic background. He believed that men deceived themselves to the very end: "Our refuge is in stupidity, in drunkenness of all kinds, in lies, in beliefs, in murder, thieving, reforming—in negation, in contempt. . . . There is no morality, no knowledge and no hope; there is only the consciousness of ourselves which drives us about a world that whether seen in a convex or a concave mirror is always but a vain and floating appearance" (To Graham, Jan. 31, 1898, Dartmouth U. Library).

The irony of the story comes full turn. Returning from the world of the dead, Marlow—our twentieth-century Everyman—cannot admit the full impact of the indecency he has witnessed, of the feelings he has experienced. Even this most honest of men must disguise what he has seen and felt. Like a politician he must bed down with lies. Only Conrad, who is outside both Marlow and Kurtz, can admit the truth, can limn the lie and see it as a lie. Only the artist, and his art, can triumph; all else is dragged down or forced to exist by virtue of untruths. Marlow, the narrator, controlled in turn by Conrad, the creator, can transform the horror of his experience into the human terms necessary for continued life. Conrad has succeeded in constructing a form which can, so to speak, hold the horror at arm's length and yet also touch us deeply.

In this and other respects, "Heart of Darkness" is a masterpiece of concealment. Just as Marlow has concealed from himself the true nature of his own needs, so too we can find concealment—in art, in nature, in people—in virtually every other aspect of the novella. The jungle itself, that vast protective camouflage barring the light of sun and sky, masks and hides, becoming part of the psychological as well as the physical landscape. Like the dream content, it forms itself around distortion, condensation, and displacement.

Post-Darwinian and overpowering, the jungle is not Wordsworth's gentle landscape, by no means the type of nature which gives strength and support in our darkest hours. Rather, it runs parallel to our anxieties, becomes the repository of our fears. The darkness of the jungle approximates darkness everywhere, adumbrating the blackness of Conrad's humor, the despair of his irony.

The persistence of the color sets the tone and elicits our response. We first meet the Romans, who penetrate *their* Congo—the English swamp, the savage Thames. Then we encounter the women in the Brussels office who knit black wool, suitable for Fates who send gladiators out to die in the jungle for the glory of empire. There are, we remember, only two Fates—Clotho and Lachesis—for the presence of the third, Atropos, would indicate Marlow's death. Their black is indeed morbid against Brussels as a "whited sepulchre." Later, when Kurtz paints in oils, he represents a woman, draped and blindfolded, carrying a torch, all against the somber background. She emerges from the dark, but only partially, for dark nourishes her. She is, in fact, a symbolic Kurtz—one contiguous with and defined by blackness. Then, just before Kurtz dies, he lies in dim light awaiting the end, despair writhing on his face, the blackness of the past merging with the mystery of the future. Once dead, Kurtz returns to the black of the Congo, his epitaph spoken by the manager's boy: "Mistah Kurtz—he dead."

The sarcastic understatement of the boy, his cruel indifference to Kurtz's prestige, all stress the contrast between Kurtz's desires and the blackness which receives him. The jungle itself will conceal him. Beyond every wish is the force of fate, the dark power which is both within and without, psychological needs and physical consequences. "Mistah Kurtz—he dead" becomes the epitaph of all those who die in jungles, their careers curtly reviewed in the contemptuous words of the boy, a bleak and black destiny.

Attached to each of these events—Kurtz's final words, his death, the report by the manager's boy, the darkness surrounding all, the frantic run out of the Congo, the meeting with Kurtz's Brussels fiancée—connected to all such events is the shimmer and nightmare of dream, Conrad's definition of modern life. No less than Kafka, he saw existence as forms of unreality stubbled with real events. And no little part of the dream-like substance of the tale is the Russian follower of Kurtz, like Marlow a mariner. Dressed in motley, he seems a figure from another world, and yet with his ludicrous appearance he is a perfect symbol for Marlow's Congo experience. Befitting someone who worships Kurtz like a god, the Russian forgives his worst behavior and argues that a common man like himself needs someone to follow. He is persuaded that Kurtz's will to power draws in all those less capable, conveys hope and substance to them.

There is, in his view, a void in every man that only someone like Kurtz can fill. Without Kurtz, the sailor says, he is nothing. "He made me see things—things." His ordinariness is balanced by Kurtz's superiority—every disciple needs a god. Like the natives, like the superb native mistress who forgives Kurtz everything, the sailor follows power. Conrad's prescience was never more trenchant.

To Marlow's accusation that Kurtz is insane, simply mad, the Russian offers Kurtz's great intelligence, his ability to talk brilliantly, his charismatic qualities. To our objection that the sailor himself is mad, Conrad offers his influence upon Marlow—he strikes in Marlow precisely the note of love-hate that Conrad's narrator has come to feel for Kurtz. Although Marlow would like to anchor himself solidly in the Russian's sea manual and reject the vapidity of the Russian, he too is drawn into Kurtz's orbit. He senses what the sailor voices.

In this strangely insane world, all alignments defy logic. Loyalties, beliefs, love, women themselves take on new shapes and attractions. Marlow, that neuter bachelor, is fascinated by the jungle woman, by her wanton, demanding display of sex, by the "fecund and mysterious life" she embodies, by the deliberate provocation of her measured walk. He is further drawn to her sense of reality; without illusion, without question, she accepts Kurtz for what he is, as integrated with the very savagery which enfolds her.

For Marlow the pull of the primitive comes full circle. Again and again, he breaks off his narrative to assure his listeners that all this really happened. Even while he talks, this modern mariner, he must convey the depth of his experience, try to convince that it was as profound as he claims. Marlow knows what happened—yet to find the precise words is almost impossible. Returning from the dead, like Eliot's Prufrock, he now has to convince his audience that there is really a hell.

The problem of Marlow, as we saw earlier, is the problem of Conrad's art: to communicate the weight and depth of an experience which is uniquely felt. Some of the criticism of Conrad's treatment, particularly F. R. Leavis's, has been directed toward his "excessive" use of descriptives to suggest mysteriousness and unspeakable events. Possibly in some areas the language is too heavy, but to labor this point is to lose sight of the story as a whole. One might, in fact, argue the very opposite: that the words—adjectives and all—beat upon us, creating drum-like rhythms entirely appropriate to the thick texture of the jungle, a more sophisticated version of Vachel Lindsay's "Congo." When one confronts the artistry of the complete piece, Conrad's reliance on verbal embellishment appears a minor consideration.

The novella in fact has form: from the opening frame with Marlow's somewhat ingenuous listeners, to the closing sequence, with Kurtz's innocent fiancée confirming her illusions. The use of a first-person narrative, through the agency of Marlow, was necessary so that Conrad could gain aesthetic distance and the reader could identify with an average man thrown into an abnormal situation. We must, Conrad realized, go through it with him and Marlow. Lacking the narrator, the story would appear too distant from the immediate experience—as though it had happened and was now over, like ancient history. From this safe distance, everyone was saved, and the evil force, Kurtz, rightfully had perished. But that is not at all Conrad's story; to make a morality play out of the tale is to destroy its felt sense. The story is concerned with hidden terrors in the normal heart, with the attractions of the unspeakable which we all experience, with the sense of power we wish to exert or identify with, ultimately with the underground existence each sentient being recognizes in himself. In this respect, Marlow as direct participant through his narration becomes indispensable.

So, too, in other respects did Conrad work out the shape of the story, in large and in details: through doubling of scenes and characters, through repetition, analogy, duplicating images, through differences of tone. From the beginning, when the ancient Romans on the Thames are contrasted with the modern Europeans on the Congo, Conrad used heightening and foreshortening, contrast and comparison to give the novella form. Most obviously, Marlow's peaceful setting on the *Nellie* is set off against his nightmarish Congo riverboat setting; in a different way, Kurtz's two fiancées are contrasted, each one standing for certain values, indeed for entire cultures, in conflict; further, the jungle is set off against the river, with jungle as death, river as possible relief; in another way, Kurtz is compared with other forms of evil, with the deceptive smoothness of the station manager, with the hypocrisy of the pilgrims; the pilgrims in turn are ironically compared with the savages they condemn, with the pilgrims less Christian than the pagan natives; within the natives, the tribal savages are contrasted with those exposed to civilization, detribalized as it were, the latter already full of wiles and deceit; light and dark, the painter's chiaroscuro, hover over the entire story, no less important here than in Milton's Christian epic; day dream and night dream form contrasts, worked out in the play between expectation and consequence, between professed ideals and realistic behavior, between Kurtz's humanitarianism and his barbarism, between Marlow's middle-class sense of English justice and the Congo reality, between the fluctuating love-and-hate which fill both Kurtz and Marlow.

Out of the infinite possibilities facing Conrad, he chose these to give unity to his language and ideas. Such devices shape our thoughts and give form to our responses; they, too, become the substance of our awareness. Only in *Nostromo*, with his use of silver, or in *The Secret Agent*, with London city streets, did Conrad find comparable central images to the Congo.

To discover the rightful place of "Heart of Darkness" in European culture, we must leave English literature and compare it with Dostoyevsky's *Notes from Underground*, Kafka's *Metamorphosis*, Thomas Mann's *Death in Venice*, Camus' *The Stranger*—all relatively short fiction concerned with underground men in an underground existence who become, through force of character or vision of art, suffering creatures outside the mainstream of society. This is typically continental fiction, not English—Conrad's vision remained Slavic. At the heart of all is an anarchy that repels and attracts, where one toys with the unimaginable and contemplates mysterious rites, where one defies the edicts of civilization and suffers secretly.

What makes this story so impressive is Conrad's ability to focus on the Kurtz-Marlow polarity as a definition of our times. European history as well as the history of individual men can be read more clearly in the light of Conrad's art; for he tells us that the most dutiful of men, a Marlow, can be led to the brink of savagery and brutality if the will to power touches him; that the most idealistic of men, Kurtz, can become a sadistic murderer; that the dirty work of this world is carried out by men whose reputations are preserved by lies. Conrad's moral tale becomes, in several respects, our story, the only way we can read history and each other. Hannah Arendt's definition of the "banality of evil," the nihilism of the average man, is fully relevant. It is a terrible story.

Dorothy Van Ghent

Nostromo

The subject of *Nostromo* is the guardianship of a treasure, a simple and fateful subject common throughout folklore. In this novel, the material form of the treasure is the silver of the San Tomé mine, in the republic of Costaguana, on the west coast of South America. The mine belongs, as a permanent concession, to the English family of Goulds; but successive civil wars, which have laid waste the land, have destroyed the workings of the mine. Charles Gould, an experienced mining engineer, sets out to rehabilitate it with the aid of North American capital. It becomes a financial success, and its success brings about the peace and order necessary for sustained economic enterprise. But when the main action of the story opens, a new political revolution, motivated by greed for the mine's riches, threatens the established order with bloodshed and anarchy.

Conrad's most fertile invention in *Nostromo* is to adapt the legendary idea of the mysterious potency of a treasure to the conditions of a frontier country in a modern period of colonial imperialism. In folklore a treasure is always a powerful *mana*-object that tests the characters of men; it confers great benefits, but only those with the highest physical and moral courage, and the deepest spiritual insight, are able to recognize its true nature and to use it properly. In a story with a modern milieu, the treasure can be quite concretely the chief industrial resource of a country—a rich silver mine—and yet, through the way men interpret its potential uses, it can arouse the most violent and disparate

From Nostromo: A Tale of the Seaboard *by Joseph Conrad. Introduction by Dorothy Van Ghent. Introduction copyright © 1961 by Holt, Rinehart and Winston, Inc. Reprinted by permission of Holt, Rinehart and Winston, Inc.*

human responses, from crude appetite to passionate idealism. Actually, everybody in Conrad's story has a different attitude toward the silver of the mine. To some it is an opportunity for loot. To others, it is the material "fact" that has made legal security and good government possible—possible, at least, until revolution again threatens. To Charles Gould, it has a very personal meaning. His father had been forced by corrupt and impotent governments to pay ruinous royalties on the then worthless property, and had died from outrage at such a perversion of justice. Gould has come under the fascination of the idea that if he can make a success of the mine, it will be a "way of atonement" for his father's death. The development and protection of the mine are to him a moral necessity.

Part of the range of ambiguity in what the treasure of the mine signifies may be illustrated by those occasions when we see the silver ingots in somebody's hands. Mrs. Gould had received the first ingot from the reopened vein, and, in her devotion to her husband, the silver seemed to her to be the palpable expression of his idealism:

> . . . she had seen the first spungy lump of silver yielded to the hazards of the world by the dark depths of the Gould Concession; she had laid her unmercenary hands, with an eagerness that made them tremble, upon the first silver ingot turned out warm from the mould; and by her imaginative estimate of its power she endowed that lump of metal with a justificative conception, as though it were not a mere fact, but something far-reaching and impalpable, like the true expression of an emotion or the emergence of a principle.

The Goulds have no children. It is suggested that, with a subtle unfaithfulness to his wife, Charles Gould has allowed his redemptory idea of the mine to usurp her place in his emotions. The language in the passage above is that of a birth, of "emergence" from "dark depths." The "spungy lump," "still warm from the mould," lies in Emilia Gould's hands as a "conception," a truly immaculate conception and the only one she will know. The San Tomé mine is to make her married life barren.

Nostromo, foreman of the stevedores who load the silver for shipping north, also is seen with ingots in his hands. Nostromo's name has come to stand for absolute fidelity and incorruptibility. But in the last episode of the story, he has become a thief. He steals a few ingots at a time from the barge-load of silver he has buried on a desert island, and disposes of them secretly so that his good name will be protected while he grows rich. To Nostromo, the treasure of the mine has meant moral death, and the touch of the ingots is hateful to him. They bear "the smell of earth, of damp foliage," the smell of a dark rot in nature.

Martin Decoud, the young Creole intellectual, is the third person who is seen in physical contact with the silver. To Decoud, the treasure has finally no more meaning than any other dead weight which will help a man to drown. He puts a couple of the heavy ingots in each pocket before he commits suicide in the Golfo Placido.

In even so slight a sketch, more than one major folklore element may be seen. There is not only the treasure itself—which in myth and fairy tale may be a golden fleece, the golden apples of the Hesperides, a horse or hound with supernatural powers, the Holy Grail, or other variations on the idea of a treasure. There is also, in the part played by Charles Gould, the motif of the "stranger knight" who comes to a "waste land," and who, because of his moral purity, is able to rehabilitate the land. Gould is always described as extremely foreign-looking, with his thin, blazingly red face and fiery moustaches; he comes from abroad (his youth was spent in Europe); he rescues the treasure of the land from the forces of corruption, and thereby brings about peace and prosperity. In a fairy tale, when the knight has accomplished his mission, he becomes the "good king" and reigns happily ever after. Gould is called the "king" of the province where the mine is located—El Rey de Sulaco. But he does not reign happily ever after. Apparently there was something wrong with his interpretation of the use of the treasure, for the same old troubles of corrupt intrigue, war, and widespread ruin appear again in the land.

In fairy tales where a treasure is the central emblem, a fairy princess is almost always associated with it, so closely that she may be looked upon as an essential part of the treasure itself. The "stranger knight's" marriage with the fairy princess is the crown of his successes. Their union is a traditional image of union and communion between people. The motif of marriage is one significant indication that the treasure in the fairy tale is more than a material thing; it is a thing with spiritual powers, and one of its mysterious significances is fulfillment in human communion. Several times Conrad describes Emilia Gould as "fairy-like," with her masses of fair hair, the rich rings on her fingers and lace on her wrists, "gracious, small, and fairy-like, before the glittering tea-set." The sterile relationship between Charles Gould and his wife is one of the important variations Conrad makes on a legendary model. This we shall examine a little more closely later.

All of the other people in *Nostromo* may be seen in terms of various tropisms of human desire when tested by the treasure—a treasure always ambiguous because it shows itself to the characters only in forms complementary to "the secret purposes of their hearts revealed amongst the bitter necessities of the time." The ordeal that each undergoes, when his deepest attitude toward the treasure is tested, forms the action of the novel.

The "ordeal" is a constant element of stories formed on the kind of model we are considering. Mortal dangers must be gone through by the adventurer who would win the benefits that a treasure can confer. This motif is found in the most sophisticated literature—like Conrad's *Nostromo*—as well as in naive folklore, simply because it represents the arduous necessities of man's work in fulfilling his needs and desires. It will be helpful to consider, in a rather simple fairy tale, the ordeal gone through by a character who desires to win a treasure, so that the complex action of Conrad's novel may be more readily grasped. The ancient Irish fairy tale about Conn-Eda will serve.[1] In this tale, the ordeal has three phases (each phase is found also in Conrad's novel). The hero, who starts out pure of heart, must, before he can command the treasure and become the "good king," pass these three tests: he must face wisely and courageously the destructive forces of nature, the evil in other people, and the evil in himself.

The queen, Conn-Eda's mother, died. His father, the king, married another woman—wicked, as all stepmothers in fairy tales are wicked. The wicked stepmother laid the good and innocent young prince under a magic forfeit, by which he was obliged to go on a deadly journey to fairyland, to obtain a treasure there. Conn-Eda asked the advice of the animals, and was told to take a little shaggy horse and to follow a rolling iron ball. He trusts, that is, to instinct (the little shaggy horse) and the laws of nature (the iron ball follows the law of gravity). But Conn-Eda, though young and innocent, has physical discipline, and he is brave. When raging water-serpents attack him, he skillfully throws them chunks of meat which the little shaggy horse carries in his ears for such an emergency. When he has to cross a mountain of fire, he makes the terrible leap through the flames courageously, and though he is scorched nearly to death, the horse has a bottle of medicine in his ear that heals the wounds, and Conn-Eda manages to go on. His worst ordeal comes at the gates of fairyland, where the little shaggy horse tells him he must kill his faithful animal companion with a knife, if they are to avoid an even greater evil. Conn-Eda has learned the evil in people, from his wicked stepmother, and the destructiveness in nature, from the water-serpents and the fire-mountain; now he is required to learn the evil of which he himself is capable. He refuses, weeping, to kill his

[1] I owe the interpretation of the story of Conn-Eda to Heinrich Zimmer's *The King and the Corpse,* edited by Joseph Campbell.

animal friend, but somehow the knife moves of itself in his hand, and the little horse lies dead. From its carcass springs a beautiful fairy prince. He helps Conn-Eda obtain the treasure and a fairy princess for his bride; the wicked stepmother falls dead from spite; and Conn-Eda's reign over his land is wise and just, the best in all Ireland.

The fairy prince who springs from the carcass of the shaggy horse can be interpreted metaphorically as representing Conn-Eda himself, after he has passed the ordeals and acquired from them the wisdom to rule. It is significant that Conn-Eda has both his father's and his mother's names—Conn and Eda; for in his nature he preserves both the humble, cherishing maternal principle, and the aggressive, rational paternal principle. Though he starts out innocent on his adventure, he has the humility to trust to instinct, such as the animals have; and he has the fortitude and discipline that a man must have to face the elemental forces of nature (that is why his wounds, though terrible, are again and again healed by the magic medicine). He wins, in the most difficult way, the experience necessary for the application of reason and for aggressive command, such as a king must have. But he is able, in the end, to integrate all of these qualities. "Reborn" from the ordeals of external evil and the deepest self-knowledge, he is now wise enough to become the guardian of the treasure of fairyland. The treasure of fairyland—the good of life, the goal of desire—is finally seen to be within and not without: it is the wisdom Conn-Eda has gained.

Let us trace the phases of the ordeal in *Nostromo*. Of evidently great importance in Conrad's design is the man Nostromo himself, who gives the title to the book, and whose name constantly occurs as leit-motif even when he is not in the foreground of the action. That Nostromo's character and role should have primary importance seems, at first glance, out of keeping with Conrad's habitual concern with subtle problems of conscience, for Nostromo does not have any subtlety of conscience to make him psychologically interesting in the way Conrad's principal characters usually are. He is called the "natural man," the "Man of the People," and his lack of a cultivated conscience is precisely the reason for his importance in this novel that is broadly representative of the human condition: for the great multitudes of men everywhere are without benefit of the cultivated conscience. Nostromo presents in clear relief the first and elemental phase of the human ordeal, the facing of the primitive tests of nature. His great achievements lie in the world of nature, which he can master because he is virile and brave and physically skillful. These Adamic qualities are implicit in the poetic image of his awakening after his swim from the sunken barge:

Nostromo woke up from a fourteen-hours' sleep and arose full length from his lair in the long grass. He stood knee-deep among the whispering undulations of the green blades, with the lost air of a man just born into the world. Handsome, robust, and supple, he threw back his head, flung his arms open, and stretched himself with a slow twist of the waist and a leisurely growling yawn of white teeth; as natural and free from evil in the moment of waking as a magnificent and unconscious wild beast. Then, in the suddenly steadied glance fixed upon nothing from under a forced frown, appeared the man.

But the world in which Nostromo lives is not the Adamic world, "natural and free from evil." It is, rather, a frontier world, where a sleepy, pastoral Campo has been invaded by industrialism, bringing with it all the complex energies, confusion of racial histories and attitudes, and moral anxieties that an industrial revolution introduces to a pastoral colonial people. In this frontier setting, the natural tests of manhood are still vitally necessary, and Nostromo passes these valiantly—tests of the sea and the mountains, and those which give a man command over the primitive passions and appetites of other men. But, tragically, ability to pass these tests is not enough.

Nostromo's superb natural gifts have their "ideal" and summary form in the virtue of fidelity—the virtue that relates him ethically to other men. But the men to whom he is bound in fidelity are men who belong to the invading industrial front—the San Tomé mine, the North American silver and iron interests, the European shipping and railway interests that have made capital investments in Costaguana. These men are involved in a vastly complicated enterprise whose potential for either good or evil is beyond the understanding of the "natural man," who has only instinct and virile pride to guide him. When revolutionary anarchy threatens the industrial interests, Nostromo is entrusted with a silver shipment, to be taken out to sea and beyond the reach of the rioters in the city. It is his great ordeal, the most "desperate affair" of his life, and he gives to it all his courage, all his skill, all his fidelity. But, afterwards, he learns that, in the complication of events, it actually mattered very little whether the silver was saved or whether it sank to the bottom of the sea. Nostromo had risked his life for nothing; his fidelity had meant nothing. His sense of the meaning of his own identity is completely baffled, for it has been undervalued by the men to whom he was faithful. Only the silver remains as a palpable fact to be trusted. Faithful to the silver, Nostromo becomes a thief.

He dies with "the bewildered conviction of having been betrayed"—as Adam himself, emerged without preparation out of the simple garden of nature into the human world of sin and death, must have died with the same sense of having been betrayed and "hardly knowing by what or by whom." The other figures in the novel, all caught in the "bitter necessities" of the frontier state, gain their plastic, significant relief from Nostromo's presence, the presence of the "natural man" whose primitive endowments are the base for any more evolved morality. Therefore his name is uttered again and again, as that of the "indispensable man" upon whom all the other characters are dependent in one way or another. Pacing slowly on his silver-grey mare through the night streets, his face muffled mysteriously by his sombrero, he is the man in the background, whose ancestry is older than civilization, and who has not even a proper kind of Christian name.

Charles Gould has his own unquestionable courage, his skill as a mining engineer, and his authority in commanding men to his purpose. But he also has, as Nostromo has not, an understanding of the complexities of the frontier milieu where he has to do his work. To return to our fairy-tale paradigm, the actions of Gould correspond with that phase of the human ordeal which demands experience of psychological evil in others in order that the treasure of life may be understood and properly used. And yet, as with Nostromo, Gould's particular gifts are not by themselves enough.

"Charles Gould was competent because he had no illusions," we are told. Nobody could be more aware of the murderous anarchism in Costaguana politics. One of his uncles had been elected President of the province of Sulaco and afterwards was put up against a wall and shot. His father had inculcated in him since childhood his own experience of the greed and corruption of Costaguana officials, the same type of officials with whom Gould has to deal in running the mine. He is also under no illusion about the motives of the North Amerian financier who has made the working of the mine possible, the great Holroyd, the millionaire endower of churches, who expresses his faith in American capitalism this way:

> We shall be giving the word for everything—industry, trade, law, journalism, art, politics, and religion, from Cape Horn clear over to Smith's Sound, and beyond, too, if anything worth taking hold of turns up at the North Pole. And then we shall have the leisure to take in hand the outlying islands and continents of the earth. We shall run the world's business whether the world likes it or not. The world can't help it—and neither can we, I guess.

But Gould is not fooled into collaboration with anyone else's vast conceptions of destiny. The success of the San Tomé mine is an aim which is "definite in space and absolutely attainable within a limited time,'' and it makes the other man, Holroyd, with his ''insatiable imagination of conquest,'' appear ''as a dreamy idealist of no importance.'' Gould's experience prepares him to stoop for his weapons, both in using Holroyd's millions to get the mine working, and in dealing with Costaguana politicians and racketeers.

He stakes his character on the success of the mine; his moral identity is bound up with it. In this way, he feels that he has kept his own personal motive pure and independent—the motive of ''atonement'' for his father's death by redemption of the mine that had killed his father. For ''material interest'' alone he would not have touched the mine, but ''material interests'' have made success possible, and vaguely he recognizes certain social ideals that may be fulfilled along the way. ''What is wanted here is law, good faith, order, security,'' he tells his wife.

> Only let the material interests once get a firm footing and they are bound to impose the conditions on which alone they can continue to exist. That's how your money-making is justified here in the face of lawlessness and disorder. It is justified because the security which it demands must be shared with an oppressed people. A better justice will come afterwards. That's your ray of hope.

But all this—law and order, good faith, security and justice for an oppressed people—is merely incidental to Gould's personal obsession, and his sense of the sacrosanct purity of his own private intention has itself prevented him from submitting to the final ordeal of self-knowledge. His idea of father-atonement is a kind of adultery, subtly wooing him away from his wife, who is left in the isolation of a sterile marriage. At moments he seems dimly aware of this fact, but emotionally unable to face it:

> He bent over her upturned face very tenderly and a little remorsefully. . . . For a moment he felt as if the silver-mine, which had killed his father, had decoyed him farther than he meant to go; and with the roundabout logic of emotions, he felt that the worthiness of his life was bound up with success. There was no going back.

In the legendary terms that we have been using to clarify the emblematic aspects of the novel, what Gould fails to recognize is that the ''treasure'' is worthless without the ''fairy princess,'' and that in abusing his union with her he has refused the human communion that is an essential benison of the treasure. In his abstract, obsessional commitment to the father, he has lost touch with the feminine, maternal principle which cherishes for its own sake—as Emilia Gould does—"the past and the future in every passing moment of the present."

Dr. Monygham's part in the book corresponds with the third phase of the ordeal—that of self-knowledge. Long before the main action of the story starts, Dr. Monygham has suffered the experience of evil in himself—an experience analogous to that moment in the tale of Conn-Eda when the prince is called upon to kill his best friend, the little shaggy horse, and though he refuses to do so, finds that the knife nevertheless moves in his hand and the deed is done. In the time of the bloody dictator, Guzman Bento, Monygham had been tortured and confessions were extorted from him implicating some of his best friends, who were imprisoned and executed on that accusation. He bears testimony to his experience by the cicatrices on his cheeks, his damaged ankles and crooked feet. This battered personality, limping around Sulaco, has come under the spell of Emilia Gould—of "the delicate preciousness of her inner worth, partaking of a gem and a flower"—and the latent tenderness of his essentially loyal nature has unfolded to it. Whereas Charles Gould has abandoned his wife to loneliness because of his conviction that the "worthiness of his life" is bound up with the success of the mine, Dr. Monygham's sense of the *unworthiness* of his life leads him to an act of self-sacrifice by which he hopes to save Emilia Gould from a frightful disaster. In terms of our legendary model, Monygham, having learned by the ordeal of self-knowledge the helpless evil of which he is capable, has the humility to offer his life for another—and he offers it for the "fairy princess" who lives by giving herself wholly to others.

He deliberately adopts the character of a traitor. When menaces close around the mine—and not the least of these is Gould's decision to dynamite it sky-high to prevent it from falling into the hands of the revolutionary troops—he decoys a whole army out into the harbor, with the lie that Gould has sunk some of the silver there, for his own use, to be retrieved later by divers. The doctor is kept on the boat, with a noose around his neck, ready for hanging if the silver is not discovered. It is an act in which his damaged reputation serves him well, for the colonel of the army believes that Monygham would naturally betray Gould for a part of the loot. As the doctor tells himself, in bitter memory of his earlier ordeal, "I am the only one fit for that dirty work." But his ruse succeeds in relieving the besieged city.

In one way or another, for every character, the silver of the mine formulates the heart's "secret purposes," by the ordeal which each undergoes in relation to it. In Martin Decoud's case, we have something that escapes direct legendary parallel, except in an interpretive and revisionary way. What Decoud suffers may be "the greatest evil of all," which, in the Conn-Eda tale, the little shaggy horse says will befall both him and the prince if the prince refuses to take up the knife. The greatest evil of all is lack of faith in the treasure. If the treasure is the good of life, then lack of faith in it is death.

When Decoud is alone with the barge-load of silver on the Great Isabel, one of the sterile spurs of rock in the Golfo Placido, he discovers the "secret purpose" of his heart to be death. The principle of his life has been rationalism, the nineteenth- and twentieth-century heritage from the Enlightenment. For traditional rationalism, ultimate reality is the evidence of the senses, which is the raw material upon which reason works. What can reason do with the evidence of the senses, even with a pile of silver ingots beside one, on a desert island in the middle of an immense gulf where no ship passes? The Ancient Mariner had a similar problem:

> Alone, alone, all, all alone,
> Alone on a wide, wide sea!
> And never a saint took pity on
> My soul in agony.

One's senses, and what reason can make of them, become as indifferent as the sea and the sky and the rock and the silver itself. Decoud commits suicide in "the immense indifference of things."

Given the range of powerful ambiguities in the meaning of the "treasure," the opening chapter, with its purely geographic and atmospheric description of setting—the gulf of ocean, the towering Cordillera, the vast plain of the Campo, a telescopic glimpse of the town —gains profound significance. As the human action of the story is elemental, in the sense that it shows the basic patterns of human desire and endeavor, so also the setting is elemental, and is presented in the first chapter in a great hour-by-hour review as the earth makes its diurnal turning. The story is subtitled "A Tale of the Seaboard": it takes place at the edge of the sea and at the edge of the land, both of them in a perspective of immensity, under the unvarying cyclical changes of the infinite sky, of day and night; and the town itself, where the human events take place, seems very small in this perspective —Conrad gives it a single mention in the last line of the chapter. The physical vantage point from which the scene is viewed is the middle of the Golfo Placido, presumably on a ship approaching the harbor of Sulaco, and the view is dominated by the gulf—its cavernous vastness, the strange calms that prevail there because of the peninsular land masses enclosing it, its isolation from the more accessible trading points on the coast. Shadow, cloud, and mist keep moving out from the land over the water: at dawn, the great shadow of the Cordillera lies over it; at midday the clouds start rolling out from the valleys and the Cordillera itself disappears as if dissolved; at night the clouds smother the gulf in impenetrable darkness. As one approaches land, the Sulaco plain extends before one endlessly, overhung by dry haze, "an opal mystery of great distances." The description covers, at a precise location on the coast of South America, a twenty-four hour review of the major geographic and cosmic phenomena by which all life on the earth is oriented.

The chief dramatic action, on which are pivoted the destinies of all the characters, also takes place during a single twenty-four hour period: the night of the loading of the silver shipment to get it away from the revolutionary rioters, the dead of night with Nostromo and Decoud on the barge with the silver out in the gulf, sunset the next day and Nostromo's wakening at the old fort after swimming across the gulf, evening and his reappearance in Sulaco—and meanwhile, that same day in Sulaco, the arrival of revolutionary forces by sea, the imprisoning and questioning of Dr. Monygham as to the whereabouts of the silver, his decision to seduce the troops out of the city in search of buried plunder, and his meeting that evening with Nostromo when he persuades him to ride over the mountains for help. The book is concerned primarily with spiritual action—with the revelation, in the midst of ordeal, of the "secret purposes" in the hearts of the characters—but the ordeal itself is the dramatized action, for it is in dramatic action that the "secret purposes" are revealed. This action is temporally placed in a twenty-four hour unit of the cosmic cycle that is simply and powerfully sketched by Conrad in the first chapter as an endlessly repeated movement in the "mystery of great distances" by which human life is environed. The cosmic repetition reflects on the human events its own repetitive form, by which these events are seen as themselves eternal patterns of man's desire and endeavor.

As the dramatic action of the book is correlated with cosmic law, apprehended in the unvarying cycles of nature, so the "treasure"—the good that men seek—is correlated with spiritual law, operating in the human heart. The treasure reveals itself only as the heart interprets it. It judges the heart. Thus the strange calms of the Golfo Placido, its isolation as a place of destiny, the clouds and shadow, the luminous mists and haze, real and local as they are in time and place, are touches of the mystery that is both the human heart and the external spaces surrounding it.

In the second chapter, Conrad uses the leisurely drone of Captain Joseph Mitchell, head of the steamship post in Sulaco, to introduce sketchily the day of the riot—that day when the revolutionaries first threatened Sulaco, making it urgent that the silver of the mine, piled up in the steamship warehouse for shipment north, be loaded secretly at night and sent off—but Mitchell is telling about it years after the event. The accents are shifted, as it is pieced out in Mitchell's somewhat senile recollection. The reader scarcely apprehends what the riot was about, or that it has much importance for the novel. Overlaid by the passage of time, it is reduced now to a not very clear and—to all appearances—not very important local anecdote. This effect of temporal passage is a correlative of the great cyclical review, as of a planet turning, that the first chapter has given. There the setting of the drama was revolved in cosmic space, under the aspect of eternal repetition. Here, under the linear reduction of time, the effect is inverted and ironic.

Captain Mitchell's discourse is a device of temporal displacement to contrive varying and multiple perspectives on the action, and this device is used all through Part I and most of Part II. It is only toward the end of Part II, with the letter Decoud writes to his sister on the day of the riot, that the main action of the book begins to emerge fully into the foregound. It may be that a reader would best approach the novel by starting with Decoud's letter and reading on to the end of Part II (the night on the barge, the landing of Decoud and Nostromo on the Great Isabel), then returning to the beginning to read straight through. This suggestion will undoubtedly be unwelcome to scholars of Conrad who are concerned primarily with the "impressionistic" technique of the book. But *Nostromo* is a notoriously baffling novel to "get into," and technique can have little importance to readers who are so put off by the deviousness of the first chapters that they fail to read the book at all. Furthermore, novels of this order have a perennial vitality to which no harm can be done even if they are read backwards rather than forwards; and it may be that *Nostromo* is one of those books that profit by being read the first time middle-against-both-ends. This way, at least, one gets a more immediate grasp of the central events, which helps one to understand and evaluate more readily the shifting background of history and personal involvement which the first half of the book builds up.

Chapters three and four perform one of Conrad's wonderful modulations from vast space to intensely immediate visual detail, which make one understand more truly what he meant by saying that his task was "before all, to make you *see* . . . no more, and it is everything." The old Garibaldino, Giorgio Viola, is seen in his house—the inn named for Italian unity, "L'Italia Una"—with his wife Teresa and their two adolescent daughters. It is the day of the riot. The old warrior Giorgio is on guard; Signora Teresa sits bowed over her two girls; the windows are shuttered, there are sounds of sporadic tumult in the town, shooting, then intervals of unaccountable stillness; they are tense, waiting for Nostromo—for this family, too, is dependent on Nostromo's courage and skill, as everyone in Sulaco is. Then they hear what they know to be the sound of a horse's shoulder scraped against a shutter, for a broad area of the pencil-lines of sunlight is effaced. It is Nostromo.

> Giorgio, with tranquil movements, had been unfastening the door; the flood of light fell on Signora Teresa, with her two girls gathered to her side, a picturesque woman in a pose of maternal exaltation. Behind her the wall was dazzlingly white, and the crude colors of the Garibaldi lithograph glowed in the sunshine.

This picture is done with simple sculptural modeling, using—as Conrad has a specially keen interest in using—effects of lighting against deep shadow, to make one "see" in the optical sense, which is preliminary to any more complicated modes of seeing. The language is not very nuanced: "a picturesque woman in a pose of maternal exaltation" is generalized phrasing for the abstractly "picture-like" and "sculpture-like"; but it is functional phrasing for the image that is needed, which is an impersonal, "classical" kind of image. For this is a classical kind of family, and through them a classical typology is achieved that deepens and strengthens the comprehensive human perspective in which events in Costaguana are placed.

They are classical as almost any Italian peasant family seems to be classical, in looks, in stances and gestures, in the career of their passions. (At the end of the book, a "classical" tragedy occurs in this family, combining incest with the murder of foster-son by father.) The classical type of the Viola family is set up beside the type of the "natural man," Nostromo—whose lineage, Conrad says, is "more ancient still," for he has "the weight of countless generations behind him and no parentage to speak of . . . like the People." Whereas the classical Viola family represents a traditional response to life in terms of a fully formed, complete, and unchanging set of mores (a response that is actually, therefore, anachronous on this unstable frontier), Nostromo, as the "natural man," has no cultural base, no established set of attitudes to put him into moral relationship, whether positive or negative, with a new frontier civilization that is itself unsteady, ambiguous, inwardly disorganized. Still another contrasting perspective is achieved between old Giorgio's idealistic republicanism and the corruption and outlawry of the Costaguanan revolutionaries on this day of the riot—a mob of thieves and demagogues shouting the bloodied words of political idealism. Giorgio's republicanism is itself classical—he is a man of the "old abstract revolutions," when men suffered not for gain but "for love of all humanity."

From the vivid detail of these two chapters, Conrad modulates back to the vast panoramic setting, now of mountain and plain, and one is given a first distant view of the actual physical violence of the Costaguana revolution—the somber and amorphous underground of the action of the book. Giorgio is standing at the door of the inn, curiously, watching the plain, where the horsed rioters are stumbling in their confused and meaningless battles:

> Tall trails of dust subsided here and there. In a speckless sky the sun hung clear and blinding. Knots of men ran headlong; others made a stand; and the irregular rattle of fire-arms came rippling to his ears in the fiery, still air. Single figures on foot raced desperately. Horsemen galloped towards each other, wheeled round together, separated at speed. Giorgio saw one fall, rider and horse disappearing as if they had galloped into a chasm, and the movements of the animated scene were like the peripeties of a violent game played upon the plain by dwarfs mounted and on foot, yelling with tiny throats, under the mountain that seemed a colossal embodiment of silence.

It is like a battle scene out of Paolo Uccello, crowded with lances and banners and the enormous rumps of horses, all utterly and frightfully static, for the feudal battles that Uccello painted were not battles—nobody but the horses got killed—but baronial trade markets in horse-flesh, armorial banners, and hardware, So this scene of revolutionary riot, passing before the eyes of the old republican soldier, is given by the short rigid phrases a peculiarly small and static fury, for its deadly violence is also that of the horseflesh-and-hardware market.

The mindless greed and ferocity of the revolutionaries are the roiling of the abyss, the demonic underground, of this *comédie humaine*. The ordeals of the principal characters are played out on hierarchic levels, and the lowest level of all is the dark and tumultuous pit of human demonism, whose uproar is also released by desire for the "treasure." As in Dante's *Commedia*, certain monsters domineer over the abyss—like the *"gran bestia"* General Montero, military idol of the revolution, imbecile and ominous as some Aztec deity, awaiting with great flatulent nostrils the homage of the smoke of burned houses and the smell of spilled blood. Here also is that abject and random victim of the silver mine, Señor Hirsch, who had his own modest pecuniary deal to make for a part of the treasure, and who, in his blind and appalling cowardice, is unwittingly carried out to sea on a barge loaded with it. Señor Hirsch is finished off by the strapado, his senseless body leaping convulsively to the lash of the whip "like a fish on the end of a line"—an image of bestiality suitable to the gross dehumanization of the underground.

It is because of the primitive threat of the abyss, where appetite, fear, and passion rage without control, that the grave simple virtues of courage and fidelity are so important in the book. There is need for staunch guardians of the city, the mine, the villages where the mine workers live, and the poor Indios of the Campo. The men who have this role wear the marks of old and fierce campaigns on their bodies—men like General Barrios, with a grotesque black patch over his eye, and Father Corbelán, whose scarred cheeks suggest "something unlawful behind his priesthood, the idea of a chaplain of bandits." Like Nostromo, these men are brave, but unlike Nostromo, they serve the traditional functions of the military and the church; their fidelity is grounded in their profession, and does not run the subjective risk that Nostromo's does. Nostromo, alone in the book, is a tragic figure, thrown with full force on a personal destiny, in which the essential choice of his manhood is enacted in opposition to a mysterious historical necessity beyond his comprehension. As the "natural man," his is the tragic figure of mankind, facing the ambiguities of history with no equipment but the instinct of survival and the pride of being a man.

And yet, despite the tragic view of life that the book contains, it is a "comedy." It is a comedy in the Dantean and the Balzacian sense, signifying a drama in which all the representative forms of human action are shown as recurrent and resurgent, played out on a cosmic scene that stretches from the abyss of demonic egoism to the angelic level of selfless communion. Nobody really achieves the "treasure," that integration of virtue and wisdom which gives command of the good of life, for this is historical realism and not emblematic legend. Even Dr. Monygham is the slave of his own experience, which he has separated unnaturally from the ordeals of other men. Emilia Gould, who represents the highest benison of the treasure, is the most lonely person in the book, for her gift is the hardest of all to recognize.

Unlike gold—which corresponds alchemically to the sun's fire, the light of day and reason—silver is a nocturnal metal, correspondent to the moon, to emotion and imagination. The "treasure," whose emblem is silver, is misprized if it is thought to be any abstract ideal or truth (as

Charles Gould thought it to be), or any theory of history that one might try to find in the story. The book shows on a vast scale the recurrence of the human ordeal and the resurgence of desire. It ends in moonlight, the brilliance of the moon lying like a bar of silver on the horizon, and with a cry of faith into the night.

Robert Wooster Stallman

Time and The Secret Agent[1]

> *"I suppose you know that the world is selfish, I mean the majority of the people in it, often unconsciously I must admit, and especially people with a mission, with a fixed idea, with some fantastic object in view, or even with only some fantastic illusion."*—The Arrow of Gold, II, p. 1

> *A man haunted by a fixed idea is insane. He is dangerous even if that idea is an idea of justice. . . .* —Nostromo, p. 369

I

Though *The Secret Agent* is one of the most cryptographic works in all British fiction, Conrad perversely appended to it the subtitle: "A Simple Tale." The only thing simple in it is the simpleton Stevie, and even he is rather a complicated character. Perhaps it's Conrad's bogus subtitle—A Simple Tale!—that has beguiled Conrad's critics and unwary readers into the trap of dismissing *The Secret Agent*—one of his

[1]Quotations from *The Secret Agent* derive from the Dent Collected Edition of Conrad's works.

Reprinted with the permission of Robert Wooster Stallman, from The Houses That James Built © *Michigan State University Press, 1961.*

richest works of art—as having no more claim to merit than as an excellent example of detective fiction (the critic is Ernest Baker), "a good Hitchcock thriller" (W. T. Webster), or as an example of the political fable (Irving Howe). A splendid book, one critic has conceded, but it is a book "in the same class as *Tono Bungay* and *The Old Wives' Tale.*" F. R. Leavis has not so much as scratched the surface of this book, but he does recognize it as "indubitably a classic and a masterpiece, and it doesn't answer to the notion at all —which is perhaps why it appears to have had nothing like due recognition." How can it possibly earn due recognition as long as its hidden meaning passes unnoticed?

All's chaos and confusion; all's incongruous and irrational, but nevertheless logic designs the structure of *The Secret Agent*. One critic attributes "the horror of the tale" to the notion that ordinary reason cannot comprehend the dialectic of evil, and he concludes that "the whole chain of circumstances defies the logic of thought." (Paul L. Wiley, *Conrad's Measure of Man,* 1954, p. 109.) No work of art defies the logic of thought. A cryptographic work of art gets itself read only by the cryptographic reader. What Marlow says of Jim's plight in *Lord Jim* applies to *The Secret Agent:* "There is to my mind a sort of profound and terrifying logic to it."

As *The Secret Agent* is among Conrad's less well known works, though it is among his greatest, a brief summary may be useful to the reader. The story, to quote Miss Bradbrook's summary (*Joseph Conrad: Poland's English Genius,* 1941, p. 48),

> has for its main event a "senseless outrage" staged by Verloc, the *agent provocateur,* which unexpectedly involves the death of his feebleminded young brother-in-law. Mrs. Verloc, whose maternal passion for Stevie is the mainspring of her simple existence, and who has never suspected her husband's activities, kills Verloc, and then in blind terror puts herself into the hands of one of the revolutionary party [Comrade Ossipon], who leaves her stranded on the Calais steamer. She throws herself overboard in despair. Such is the story, but its melodramatic events are all told with a deliberate and consistent foreshortening. They are described purely and externally, and always with an ironic overtone.

The story had its inception in an incident reported to Conrad by Ford Madox Ford, an attempt to destroy Greenwich Observatory with a bomb. The bomb-thrower, who was half an idiot, succeeded only in blowing himself to pieces. His sister afterwards committed suicide. From this germinal seed Conrad constructed the sordid domestic world of the Verlocs, and it may be noted (to quote Oliver Warner's *Joseph*

Conrad, 1951) that such a *milieu* is seldom met with elsewhere in Conrad. The whole book is conceived in an ironical temper, as Conrad defined it in a letter to R. B. Cunninghame Graham (October 7, 1907): "a sustained effort in ironical treatment of a melodramatic subject." While different from the majority of Conrad's works, the difference, as Douglas Hewitt observes, is on the surface: "it is a difference of presentation rather than of the preoccupations which lie at the back of it. There is no central character in whom the problems of value are worked out, no character who is the focal point of the moral issues involved. It is more nearly a comedy than any other novel of Conrad—a comedy which is intensely serious and in which the pity and scorn of which he speaks in the 'Author's Note' are most important." The element of brutal and sordid farce, which appears also in "Heart of Darkness" and in "Falk," is here dominant (*Conrad: A Reassessment,* 1952, p. 85). Recasting the novel, Conrad later succeeded in creating a remarkable play: *The Secret Agent–A Drama in Four Acts* (1923).

What has eluded Conrad's critics is the simple fact that all time —legal time, civil time, astronomical time, and Universal Time —emanates from Greenwich Observatory *and* that Verloc's mission, in the intended bombing of Greenwich Observatory, is to destroy Time-Now, Universal Time, or life itself. Conrad's cosmic irony is exemplified in Mr. Vladimir's theory that "the blowing up of the first meridian is bound to raise a howl of execration." It's no wonder that Mr. Verloc is unnerved by Mr. Vladimir's orders—"Go for the first meridian."[2] His mission is the destruction of space and time, as the great circle of Greenwich meridian is the zero from which space is measured and time is clocked. From Greenwich zero, terrestrial longitudes are reckoned, and what are these when mapped but concentric circles? Stevie, Winnie Verloc's brother, spends his time drawing "circles, circles, circles; innumerable circles, concentric, eccentric; a corruscating whirl of circles that by their tangled multitude of repeated curves, uniformity of form, and confusion of intersecting lines suggested a rendering of cosmic chaos, the symbol of a mad art attempting the inconceivable" (III). * It is ironical that Stevie, the only artist in the world of *The Secret Agent,* is a half-wit.

Stevie's circles diagram the design of the book. First of all, every person in *The Secret Agent* is rendered as a circle of insularity, each

---

*The Roman numerals within parentheses refer to chapter numbers in *The Secret Agent* [editor's note].

[2] The world "in *The Secret Agent* appears stricken with moral insanity which breaks out in the incomprehensible attack on the fifth [*sic*] meridian," Paul L. Wiley writes in *Conrad's Measure of Man,* p. 107. Perhaps it is because he has his meridians mixed that the attack seems to him incomprehensible.

insulated from another by his own self-love, by self-illusions and fixed ideas or theories, while like eccentric circles each selfhood impinges upon another by sharing some portion of its attributes, outlook, or theory. The novel presents an ironic concatenation of theories or illusions shocked to zero by the impingements of reality, by the impingements of the unexpected and the unpredictable.

Ex-convict Michaelis—"round like a tub," having been fattened during fifteen years in a damp and lightless prison at the expense of an outraged society—expounds in Adolf Verloc's shop certain theories constituting his apostolic credo; but when his tirade is cut short by a harsh laugh from Comrade Ossipon, Michaelis thereupon falls into silence—and Stevie into drawing circles. What they all have in common is an abhorrence of ideas which contradict and upset their own. Insularity characterizes everyone in the novel. "There was no young man of his age in London more willing and docile than Stephen, she affirmed; none more affectionate and ready to please, and even useful, as long as people did not upset his poor head." Theories excite the irrational Stevie; they make him mad! Michaelis talks to himself, only to himself, "indifferent to the sympathy or hostility of his hearers, indifferent indeed to their presence, from the habit he had acquired of thinking aloud hopefully in the solitude of the four white-washed walls of his cell . . . sinister and ugly like a colossal mortuary for the socially drowned" (III). The mere fact of "hearing another voice" disconcerted Michaelis painfully; he was no good at discussion.

It was the theory of violence which Karl Yundt declared in refutation of Michaelis' optimism that excited Stevie into drawing circles, as though to erect order out of chaos. More theorist than terrorist, Yundt is optimistic in his pessimism: "I have always dreamed," he mouthed fiercely,

> of a band of men absolute in their resolve to discard all scruples in the choice of means, strong enough to give themselves frankly the name of destroyers, and free from the taint of that resigned pessimism which rots the world. No pity for anything on earth, including themselves, and death enlisted for good and all in the service of humanity—that is what I would have liked to see (III).

Ironically, "The famous terrorist had never in his life raised personally as much as his little finger against the social edifice." Each revolutionist accuses the other of being pessimistic about the future, and each outdoes the other in optimistic theories aimed at the destruction of the world as it is. Michaelis' "optimism began to flow from his lips. He saw Capitalism doomed in its cradle, born with the poison of the principle of competition in its system. The great capitalists devouring the little capitalists . . . and in the madness of self-aggrandizement only preparing, organizing, enriching, making ready the lawful inheritance of the suffering proletariat'' (III). As the toothless terrorist Yundt puts it, the nature of our present economic conditions is cannibalistic. Cannibalism and gluttony are evoked in the image of Adolf Verloc butchering some meat for his supper on the night of Stevie's slaughter: "The piece of roast beef, laid out in the likeness of funeral baked meats for Stevie's obsequies, offered itself largely to his notice. And Mr. Verloc again partook. He partook ravenously, without restraint and decency'' (XI). Cannibalism is suggested by the butcher knife in the Verloc household. The knife-motif is recurrent throughout the novel and culminates in the murder scene—and again by "the knife of infuriated revolutionists,'' which is the knife that Verloc fears. After the explosion at Greenwich Park nothing is left of Stevie but a mound of rags "concealing what might have been an accumulation of raw material for a cannibal feast'' (V).

Although the theories of the revolutionists amount to cannibalism, they profess confidence in the future of life on this globe. "The humanitarian hopes of the mild Michaelis tended not towards utter destruction, but merely towards the complete economic ruin of the system.'' The patroness of Michaelis supports him (in a cottage at Greenwich Park) and believes in his Theory of the Future. She fails to see that his theory has a hole in it. Universal ruin, as prophesied by Michaelis, "would leave the social values untouched. The disappearance of the last piece of money could not affect people of position. She could not conceive how it could affect her position, for instance'' (VI). Mr. Verloc, who himself has no future, is Vice-President of the Future of the Proletariat—which likewise has no future. Nobody has any future because nobody shares life or time now; nobody enjoys life except the moron Ossipon, who regards himself as quite the lady-killer. Professor X scorns Michaelis, the visionary prophet of the future. " 'Prophecy! What's the good of thinking what will be.' He raised his glass. 'To the destruction of what is,' he said, calmly'' (XII).[3] As Conrad remarks, "perverse unreason has its own logical processes''—a remark which is

[3]In Robert Payne's *The Terrorists: The Story of the Forerunners of Stalin* (1957), Sergey Nachayev, one of the terrorists who flung bombs and wrote inflammatory pamphlets, who believed in science and little else, was consumed by "a pure thirst for destruction.'' His self-abnegation and monstrous insolence and arrogance remind us of Conrad's Professor X. "Our task,'' said Nachayev, "is total, terrible, universal and merciless destruction.''

exemplified in the person of Professor X, who has a built-in-bomb secured to his emaciated body, a sane man insanely equipped to blow himself instantaneously into eternity. The great word that Michaelis utters is *Patience,* and with that word we've epitomized the character of Professor X, for he exercises heroic patience in his lifelong quest to perfect the detonator—one which doesn't go off at the wrong time! Perverse unreason is exemplified also by Michaelis, the Apostle, who is—like Stevie—a harmless creature and "a little mad." His ideas are "inaccessible to reasoning."

"You wouldn't deceive an idiot," says Mr. Vladimir (First Secretary of the Russian Embassy) to Secret Agent Verloc, whereupon Verloc proceeds to deceive the idiot Stevie. Stevie is blown to shreds on the road to Greenwich Observatory while carrying a varnish-can containing a bomb prepared by Professor X, and at the sight of what's left of him an idiotic constable opines "with stolid simplicity: 'He's all there. Every bit of him . . .' " (V). Poor Stevie never was all there, but then neither is Professor X. It is he, rather than the idiot Stevie, who represents madness personified. "Lunatic!" he shouts at Michaelis, and lunatic is Verloc's label for his wife just before she murders him. Perverse unreason is exemplified by Winnie Verloc, when after the murder she "imagined her incoherence to be clearness itself" (XII). Or again by Mr. Vladimir, whose "wit consisted in discovering droll connections between incongruous ideas" (II). Like Professor X, Vladimir is obsessed by a theory of bomb-throwing—if only "one could throw a bomb into pure mathematics." Mr. Vladimir's theory is to attack *the* sacrosanct fetish of our society. It's not religion, not art, not royalty; it's science. Therefore have a go at astronomy! "Such an outrage combines the greatest possible regard for humanity with the most alarming display of ferocious imbecility."

In the final scene at the Silenus beer-hall the "incorruptible Professor" echoes the sham journalistic sentiment of the newspaper reporting the suicide of Winnie Verloc: "Madness and despair! Give me that for a lever, and I'll move the world" (XIII). He'll move it by blowing it up! Madness and despair sum up his plight as well as Winnie Verloc's, and Winnie in turn shares identity with the irrational Stevie. Just before plunging the carving knife into her husband's breast, "As if the homeless soul of Stevie had flown for shelter straight to the breast of his sister, guardian, and protector, the resemblance of her face with that of her brother grew at every step, even to the droop of the lower lip, even to the slight divergence of the eyes" (XI). Every person in *The Secret Agent* shares identity with another; each circled selfhood overlaps.

As the revolutionists depend upon conventions, so Chief Inspector Heat depends on life—whereas Professor X depends on death. "Like to like. The terrorists and the policeman both come from the same basket. Revolution, legality—countermoves in the same game" (IV). Policeman Heat and the revolutionists—they are products of the same machine ("one classed as useful and the other as noxious"). Heat "could understand the mind of a burglar, because, as a matter of fact, the mind and instincts of a burglar are of the same kind as the mind and instincts of a police officer. Both recognize the same conventions, and have a working knowledge of each other's methods and of the routine of their respective trades" (V). Law and Order versus Rebellion against Convention, these two worlds coalesce—like Stevie's eccentric circles, "repeated curves of form and confusion." This situation, the ironic center of the narrative, is expressed otherwise in the Professor's contempt: "You revolutionists . . . are the slaves of the social convention, which is afraid of you; slaves of it as much as the very police that stands up in defense of that convention. Clearly you are, since you want to revolutionize it" (IV). Thus identities overlap, one interfusing with another.

Indolence, immobility, and rotundity characterize Winnie's mother, the plump Winnie Verloc, fat and lazy Verloc, Comrade Ossipon, and Michaelis ("Round like a distended balloon"). Prison has fattened up Verloc and likewise Michaelis—"pathetic in his grotesque and incurable obesity." The swollen legs of Winnie's mother have rendered her inactive. Inactive also are the revolutionists—Yundt, Ossipon, Michaelis, and Verloc. Fat Inspector Heat has kinship with the fat revolutionists; while the Assistant Commissioner of Police—"tall and thin"—has kinship with the thin terrorists—Yundt, Professor X, and the innocent Stevie (each is afflicted with a deformity). The Professor's "stunted stature" has its parallel in the stunted mentality of Stevie—he can't remember even his own name and address! "An absurdity," as Razumov in *Under Western Eyes* reminds us, "may be the starting-point of the most dangerous complications" (III, I).

Everybody in *The Secret Agent* is a fragmented and frustrated anonymity. Nameless are Professor X, Winnie's former butcher lover, Winnie's unscrupulous and deformed mother, the clever and noncommittal Assistant Commissioner, and Secret Agent Δ (as the nameless Adolf Verloc is known in the files of the Russian Embassy). Verloc's *alias* is Prozor; and Alexander Ossipon, among women intimate with him, goes by the name of Tom; Michaelis is known as the Apostle; and the Home Secretary as Sir Ethelred, as the Presence, as the Personage, and also as The Chief. Even when Conrad's characters have names, their identity remains fragmented; Heat, Wurmt, Toodles, Lombroso—all of them lack first names. Without last names are the Patroness,[4] Sir Ethelred, Vladimir, and Stevie—named after Saint Stephen, the martyr. Everyone in *The Secret Agent* is a fragmented selfhood, anonymous or deformed. The purpose of these characteristics is to indicate their lack of vitality, their insulation from life, and their moral indolence. The insularity of Verloc's perverted and lifeless existence is signified by the triangle sign designating his nameless selfhood, and again by the triangle of the street in which his box of a house is located; by that sign of a triangle Verloc is reduced to an abstraction. "There was no sparkle of any kind on the lazy stream of his life" (XI). A lifeless automaton, Verloc has no more vitality than the poisoned atmosphere of the Russian Embassy, where nothing exists suggesting life or contact with it except a faintly buzzing housefly. "The useless fussing of that tiny, energetic organism affected unpleasantly this big man threatened in his indolence" (II).

Everything exists in contradiction of itself, and nothing is but what is not. Winnie Verloc, whom we recognize as personifying death, is also described as representing "the mystery of life." The mystery of life is, of course, simply its unpredictableness. *As the emblem of life,* Winnie Verloc is ironically handicapped by a half-wit brother, a crippled and deformed mother, an anonymous and morally perverted husband, and a lover—Comrade Ossipon—by whom she is betrayed. Life is represented in *The Secret Agent* as irrational (for example, Stevie and the Professor), unreal and devoid of vitality (Verloc), routine and dull (the Assistant Commissioner), conventional (Winnie Verloc), deformed and prostituted (Winnie's mother). The life of Winnie's mother has consisted in running what Conrad politely calls "business houses" where "queer gentlemen" boarded. One conjectures that Winnie, being a dutiful daughter to her "impotent" mother, contributed certain accommodations to these queer gentlemen. While the change from her Belgravian house to Adolf's shop affected her legs adversely, the moral

---

[4]The fixed idea possessing me during the past decade of readings of *The Secret Agent* was that the lady patroness of Michaelis, who is in fact not named in the novel, bore the name of Lady Mabel. In proofreading "Time and *The Secret Agent,*" my essay in *The Art of Joseph Conrad: A Critical Symposium* (1960), I discovered however that I had therein bestowed upon that nameless creature the title Lady Mabel. In *The Secret Agent* that title is unwarranted; she has no name, I append this note here to correct my error. Where did I get this fixed idea? Well, she *is* named Lady Mabel in Conrad's dramatized version of *The Secret Agent:* "The Secret Agent: A Drama in Four Acts" (in *Three Plays,* by Joseph Conrad. London: Methuen & Co., 1934). The present note corrects my *Texas Studies* essay.

sensibility of Winnie's mother presumably was not exactly shocked when she found herself housed in Verloc's shop of pornographic wares, as by then this Madam of Business Houses was no doubt rather familiar with them. Of all the persons in *The Secret Agent* the only one spared and protected from the author's grotesque and cosmic ironies is Winnie's mother, and what protects her is the fact of her early removal to an almshouse.

Verloc's contact with life is through Winnie, and Stevie's future depends upon her protection. Every man is supported or protected by a woman: Yundt, nursed by the woman he betrayed; Michaelis, sustained by his patroness; and Comrade Ossipon, whose selfish ego finds satisfaction in women who "put some material means into his hands." It is ironical that the Assistant Commissioner of Police is ruled by a domineering wife, a cantankerous woman who has thwarted his prospects of a career in Europe; wherefore he has nothing to look forward to but evening games of whist at the Explorer's Club. At the crisis, after the bombing at Greenwich Observatory, it is Verloc's bond of respectability that traps him—the convention of a virtuous attachment. Verloc would leave the country at once, just as the police have urged him to do, " 'only he felt certain that his wife would not even hear of going abroad. Nothing could be more characteristic of the respectable bond than that,' went on, with a touch of grimness, the Assistant Commissioner, whose own wife, too, had refused to hear of going abroad . . . 'From a certain point of view we are here in the presence of a domestic drama' " (X). By playing whist at the Club, the Assistant Commissioner is protected from facing his own domestic drama—he and his card-table cronies approach the game "in the spirit of cosufferers, as if it were indeed a drug against the secret ills of existence" (V).

Conradian irony has reduced a story about revolutionists to their domestic drama, a domestic drama which—whether located in the Verloc household or in the parlors of the Patroness—represents sanctuary from the secret ills of existence, sanctuary from life or time itself. Winnie Verloc's attempt to escape with Comrade Ossipon to the Continent, to find sanctuary there under the illusion that he is her savior and lover, is thwarted at the start—how escape an island? "The insular nature of Great Britain obtruded itself upon his notice in an odious form" (XII). Stevie's sanctuary from reality lies in the fact that his grasp of language is limited, for he knows only the names of things and ideas that are simple enough not to upset him. "Certain simple principles had been instilled into him so anxiously (on account of his 'queerness') that the mere names of certain transgressions filled him with

horror'' (VIII). Like Stevie, the Patroness and Michaelis live outside
of time or reality, of which they are as ignorant as is Sir Ethelred—he
has no time for details. "Don't go into details. I have no time for that.
. . . Spare me the details" (VII). But it is the details, concrete things
and facts, that comprise the reality of life; all else is abstraction.

Ford Madox Ford speculates that the London of *The Secret Agent*
is a city "rather of the human soul than any place in topography.
Similarly the Anarchists of *The Secret Agent* are Anarchists of Nowhere: the Enemies of any society" (*Thus to Revisit,* 1921). On the
contrary, Conrad has rooted his characters in a specific city (not just "A
City"): the London he knew intimately, far more intimately than his
friend Ford speculates; and furthermore he has utilized the actualities of
London—its streets and houses—to provide his characters analogies of
themselves or their plight. Verloc's house in Soho is located in a trian-
gular well of "blind houses and unfeeling stones" (XII). That description defines Verloc himself, unfeeling and blind to the realities. "But
Mr. Verloc was not in the least conscious of having got rusty" (II).
He's as rusty as "the rusty London sunshine struggling clear of the
London mist" to shed a lukewarm brightness into the First Secretary's
Russian Embassy room, where Conrad deposits Verloc for Chapter II.
At the outrageous hour of half-past ten in the morning—outrageous
because Verloc, a night-prowler, is as unfamiliar with the sun as he is
with life itself—Verloc departs from Soho for the Russian Embassy. He
goes westward—not towards the sun. It's "a peculiarly London sun
—against which nothing could be said except that it looked bloodshot.
. . . It hung at a moderate elevation above Hyde Park Corner with an
air of punctual and benign vigilance. The very pavement under Mr.
Verloc's feet had an old-gold tinge in that diffused light, in which
neither wall, nor tree, nor beast, nor man cast a shadow. Mr. Verloc
was going westward through a town without shadows in an atmosphere
of powdered old gold" (II). The bloodshot and shadowless sun identifies itself with Verloc. Its coppery gleams fall on the broad back of his
blue overcoat and produce "a dull effect of rustiness."

The coppery gleams and old-gold-tinged light befit Verloc's present mood of self-satisfaction. He's in a mood of opulence as he broods
on his Theory of Protection: "All these people had to be protected.
Protection is the first necessity of opulence and luxury." His theory is
upset by the contrary theory of the Russian First Secretary, a theory
having to do with destruction rather than protection. That Verloc, secret
agent, casts no shadow befits his anonymity. It signifies also that he has
no future.

Verloc casts no shadow, but he's had a shady past. It included five
years of rigorous confinement in a fortress for divulging the design of a

new British field gun, a woman having betrayed him. Verloc's shop—"a square box of a place"—is located in "a shady street . . . where the sun never shone." The insularity of Verloc's household is indicated also by the fact that news from the outside world seldom reaches Brett Street; newsboys never invade it. Verloc's shop, behind which lives the Verloc household, is a front masking his activities as *agent provocateur*. It wasn't out of love for Winnie that he transported her and her impotent mother and imbecile brother from their Belgravian house to Soho, where he set up the shop with money supplied by Winnie. He gathered that trio and their furniture "to his broad, good-natured breast" so as to provide himself thereby a protective mask. It's a shock to Verloc to be told by Mr. Vladimir that anarchists don't marry and that he has discredited himself in his world by his marriage. "This is your virtuous attachment—eh? What with one sort of attachment and another you are doing away with your usefulness" (II).

The novel begins (in Chapter II) with Verloc, the domesticated *agent provocateur,* wrenched from his habitual routine—"Mr. Verloc, going out in the morning." Verloc seldom goes out in the daytime, whereas the Professor seldom goes out at night. Like Verloc, Ossipon "slept in the sunlight." Verloc nominally left his half-wit brother-in-law in charge of the shop during the day, and then—as there was practically no business—the shop door remained closed. At night "it stood discreetly but suspiciously ajar"—for the shady customers of the shady wares, the "queer gentlemen" who "dodged in sideways, one shoulder first, as if afraid to set the bell going. The bell, hung on the door by means of a curved ribbon of steel, was difficult to circumvent. It was hopelessly cracked; but of an evening, at the slightest provocation, it clattered behind the customer with impudent virulence" (I). The bell signifies life, the sound of life vibrating in the silence of Brett Street, where the sun never shines and "all the sounds of life seemed lost as if in a triangular well of asphalt and brick" (XII). And that is why the door stands ajar for the queer customers of pornographic wares; so that they can enter without ringing the virulent bell—life, hostile to their moral and sexual impotence. When Winnie Verloc tends the shop, customers "get suddenly disconcerted at having to deal with a woman" (I). The shop bell rings, and the solitary deadness of the silent place is disturbed, stirred into life. It has an "aggressive clatter"; it disturbs Stevie until it quiets down. It also unnerves Chief Inspector Heat, the clatter of the cracked bell causing him "to spin round on his heel" (IX). Again, its clatter associates with Verloc's mood of restlessness and Stevie's nervous shuffling of his feet (VIII). When its clattering ceases, the tenants of the shop sense a vacancy, a loss (VIII). "And when the cracked bell ceased to tremble on its curved ribbon of steel *nothing stirred* near Mrs. Verloc, as if her attitude had the looking power of a spell" (IX). After murdering Verloc, Winnie is stirred to life by her chance encounter with the unscrupulous Ossipon, whose only saving attribute is his passionate nature. (Winnie's other romance was with a butcher, whom she rejected for a gentleman—whom she, in turn, butchered.) Ossipon sets the bell clattering both on his entrance to and exit from the shop, and it frightens him so much that he pins his arms to his side in "a convulsive hug." "Comrade Ossipon had no settled conception now of what was happening to him" XII). The bell shatters his stability and self-possession. Is it any wonder then that the "queer gentlemen" try to sidle past that symbolic bell?

That cracked bell associates with moods of bewilderment and confusion. At the Silenus beer-hall instead of a bell there is a mechanical piano, whose deafening din confounds the theories voiced by Ossipon and his beer-hall companion, the Professor. It's a slightly defective mechanical piano and "lonely"—executing airs unaccompanied, "a valse tune with aggressive virtuosity" (IV). Like the cracked bell with its "aggressive clatter," this "semi-grand piano" signifies life. What's life but the companion of death, each competing against the other! Death is represented by the lonely and mechanical Professor X, who is but the ghost of a human being ("I am deadly"), an automaton executing mad theories with aggressive virtuosity, eloquent but slightly cracked. So the piano plays distant airs in painfully detached notes, or else it clatters "through a mazurka in brazen impetuosity, as though a vulgar and imprudent ghost were showing off. The keys sank and rose mysteriously" (IV).

As Razumov in *Under Western Eyes* remarks: "There is nothing, no one, too insignificant, too absurd to be disregarded. . . ." It is the insignificant *things* in *The Secret Agent,* the minute particulars of life, that manifest reality; and the characteristic of these pieces of reality is their absurdity—the cracked bell, the forsaken wedding ring, the lonely mechanical piano, Verloc's round hat rocking on its crown, Stevie's coat label, the buzzing fly. All "mere trifles," but not one of these pieces of reality is too insignificant, too absurd to be disregarded. *They each signify the unpredictable,* the absurdly incongruous thing which disturbs routine existence by the sudden fact of its uncalled-for and unexpected intrusion. The nature of reality in *The Secret Agent* is irrational, incongruous, and incalculable. Take, for example, that section of London where the Russian Embassy is located—across from Chesham Square at Number 10:

With a turn to the left Mr. Verloc pursued his way along a narrow street by the side of a yellow wall which, for some inscrutable reason, had No. 1 Chesham Square written on it in black letters. Chesham Square was at least sixty yards away, and Mr. Verloc, cosmopolitan enough not to be deceived by London's topographical mysteries, held on steadily, without a sign of surprise or indignation. At last, with business-like persistency, he reached the Square, and made diagonally for the number 10. This belonged to an opposing carriage gate in a high, clean wall between two houses, of which one *rationally enough* bore the number 9 and the other was numbered 37.

Number 37 is on Chesham Square, but actually it belongs to Porthill Street. Here, as throughout the novel, the expected does not occur. Rather, what occurs is the unexpected, the irrational. There is no logical sequence to these stray and misnumbered edifices: The fact that Number 37 "belonged to Porthill Street . . . was proclaimed by an inscription placed above the ground-floor windows by whatever highly efficient authority is charged with the duty of keeping track of London's strayed houses." Let these houses get up and rearrange themselves in logical order! "Why powers are not asked of Parliament . . . for compelling those edifices to return where they belong is one of the mysteries of municipal administration" (II).

II

"Conrad's secret theory examined," F. Scott Fitzgerald wrote in his Notebooks; and the secret of Conrad's scheme? Well, he wrote the truth—"adding confusion however to his structure." Adding confusion to his structure, Conrad has dislocated the chronology of narrated events so as to shape his narrative in circular form. The circular design of *The Secret Agent* manifests Conrad's commentary on human progress, and in this Conrad is at one with Hawthorne: Progress is but circular—a spiral of concentric circles.

The event which initiates all subsequent action—namely, the explosion at Greenwich—is first made known in Chapter IV. The first three chapters present preliminary matters and serve as Prologue to the drama. The event which concludes the drama—Winnie Verloc's death by drowning—is made known by Ossipon's report of it to the Professor in the Silenus Restaurant—through a newspaper now ten days old. Likewise in Chapter IV, Stevie's death by fireworks is rendered as a reported event, and again it is made known through the newspaper which Ossipon reads to the Professor in the Silenus Restaurant: a "rosy sheet, as if flushed by the warmth of its own convictions, which were optimistic." Its account of the Greenwich affair is incomplete, and the sentimentalized newspaper report of Winnie's suicide is likewise fragmentary. Of the three main events—the explosion, the murder, and the suicide—only the murder scene is presented as a point-present action, whereas the first and the final events are reported piecemeal through multiple points of view. As the drama ends where it began, the final scene duplicating in setting and in method of presentation the scene in Chapter IV which initiates the entire action, *The Secret Agent* is designed in circular form.

Each of the three main events occurs in a single location without movement or transition to another place; hence each scene is an enclosed unit, boxed in or encircled. Other than these three enclosed actions in IV, XI, and XIII (the action in IV and in XIII is verbal), all the other scenes present an action or movement progressing from place to place, a journey which ends where it began and which therefore figures as circular. Chronologically, the narrative begins with Chapter II: Mr. Verloc leaves his shop and journeys to the Russian Embassy, and then after his interview with Mr. Vladimir he returns to the shop, where his arclike journey began. The opening phrase of the novel—"Mr. Verloc, *going out in the morning*"—is misleading, inasmuch as Mr. Verloc does not go out of the shop until the scene of Chapter II, all of Chapter I being a cutback taking us *inside* the shop. It's rather like a film run backwards; in effect, time stands still. The scene of Chapter III, Verloc's shop where the revolutionists expound their various theories, is a self-contained unit of verbal action, enclosed as in a circle. This scene occurs the night of Verloc's harrowing interview with Mr. Vladimir, and then a week elapses between Chapters III and VIII, which scene is wrenched from the chronology—in time-sequence VIII follows III. Here again the action is in circular form: from the shop Winnie's mother is taken in the "the Cab of Death" to the almshouse, Winnie and Stevie returning then to the shop where their journey began. At the beginning of Chapter IX Verloc has returned from the Continent, and ten days have elapsed since the incident of the cabman and his mistreated horse, for whom Stevie has the bizarre and "symbolic longing" to make them happy by taking them both to bed with him! In IX Verloc takes an afternoon walk with Stevie, and the next morning they again leave the shop, Verloc returning this time alone. As we knew in Chapter IV, which in time-sequence occurs a few hours after the opening parts of IX, Stevie's been blown to bits—a revelation made to Winnie by Chief Inspector Heat through her identification of Stevie's coat label. Meanwhile Verloc, who has gone out with an unidentified foreigner (the Assistant Commissioner), returns from the Continental Hotel to the shop. Thus in IX three journeys take place (each figuring in circular form, A to B and back to A).

The theme of *The Secret Agent* has to do with time—the destruction and confusion of time itself; the confused chronology of narrated events, by their disarrangement from time, effects a structure which is at one with the theme. Relocated chronologically, subsequent to Chapter IX come chapters IV, V, VI, VII, and then X, which begins where VII ends. In each of these scenes a circular action is rendered. Stevie's circles, "repeated curves" suggesting "form and confusion," diagram the design of the whole novel.

The scene of the murder (XI), which is the climax of the whole domestic drama, occurs simultaneously with the scene which concludes Chapter X. Thus as identities overlap from character to character, so likewise scenes overlap in the time-sequence, and actions circle back to their beginnings. In Chapter XII Winnie leaves the shop (having murdered her husband) and, on encountering Ossipon, she persuades him to return to the shop. Everything circles back upon itself. Actions are thus enclosed in circle form. The scenes in IV and XIII, occurring in the Silenus Restaurant, and in III and XI, occurring in the Verloc shop, present verbal actions only, gestures and words without movement from place to place; these four scenes are self-enclosed. All four of these scenes have to do with violence, theories or acts of violence. That Conrad is tinkering with the clock is hinted at in the scene of the Cab of Death: "and time itself seemed to stand still" (VIII). By backtracking the narrative progression, time is rendered as if standing still, and the same effect is created where one scene overlaps another simultaneously. The calendric span of the narrative is one month, precisely thirty-one days; but while much time elapses on the author's clock, the fact is that all the events *enacted* take place within four days.[5] In the murder scene the clock of narrated events slows down, and momentarily time seems to stand still.

In his *Joseph Conrad* (1947) Mr. Albert Guerard, Jr. opined: "We would not begrudge a hundred slow-moving pages devoted to a study of Winnie Verloc's feelings, but twenty pages sacrificed to the largely physical approach to the murder of her husband seems excessive." But this misses the intent and the significance of the whole thing. There are in fact more than thirty pages devoted to the murder, of which the

[5]One week elapses between Chapter III and the subsequent scene in VIII, ten days elapse between VIII and IX (Verloc disappears on a trip abroad), and ten days elapse between XI and the final scene in XIII. Chapter IX uses up two days; VIII one additional day; II and III comprise another additional day. Everything *happens* within these four days, beginning with the events of II–III, then VIII, then IX.

preliminaries—beginning with Verloc's irony: "You'll want all your wits about you after I am taken away" (p. 232)—consume twenty pages. It is 8:25 P.M. when Winnie, prevented by Verloc from leaving the house, feels trapped and entertains the notion of stabbing—"she wanted a knife" (p. 256). It is ten minutes to nine when, just after planting the butcher knife in her husband's "broad, good-natured breast," Mrs. Verloc "raised her head slowly and looked at the clock with inquiring mistrust" (p. 264). When next she looks up mechanically at the wooden clock, "She thought it must have stopped. She could not believe that only two minutess had passed since she had looked at it last. Of course not. It had been stopped all the time. . . . She seemed to have heard or read that clocks and watches always stopped at the moment of murder for the undoing of the murderer" (pp. 268–269). It's not only the wooden clock on the wall that has stopped, but also the author's clock—notably at the moment of the murder. What Marlow in *Lord Jim* explains—"All this happened in much less time than it takes to tell, since I am trying to interpret for you into *slow speech* the instantaneous effect of visual impressions"—describes precisely what Conrad creates in the slow prose of the murder scene—a sense of time suspended.[6]

At the signal from her recumbent spouse, "Come here" (a call "intimately known to Mrs. Verloc as the note of wooing"), "she started forward at once, as if she were still a loyal woman bound to that man by an unbroken contract." He has the fixed idea that she is still his devoted wife, and she is possessed by the "fixed idea" that he "had taken the 'poor boy' away from her in order to kill him . . . the man whom she had trusted, took the boy away to kill him!" The shock of

---

[6]In *The House of the Seven Gables* Hawthorne, in the famous death scene of Judge Pyncheon in Chapter XVIII, creates by a shift in the point-of-view the effect of a halted segment of time, a symbolic representation of a frozen moment. The parallel is Chapter XI of *The Secret Agent*. Judge Pyncheon "holds his watch in his left hand, but clutched in such a manner that you cannot see the dial plate." Time ticks on, but not Judge Pyncheon; and, as in *The Secret Agent*, the narrative progression comes to a standstill by the shift in the point-of-view. Hawthorne addresses the corpse: "Rise up, Judge Pyncheon!" A housefly alights on the dead man's forehead, and then on his chin, "and now, Heaven help us! is creeping over the bridge of his nose, towards the would-be chief magistrate's wide open eyes!" "Canst thou not brush the fly away? Art thou too swiggish?"

Hawthorne's housefly resettles in the Russian Embassy of *The Secret Agent*, where Verloc hears it buzzing against the windowpane (II). Conrad has also lifted from *The House of the Seven Gables* the shop bell, which before and after the death-scene clatters to return us from that halted segment of time to the recognition of the Moment-Now—back to time rushing on with life. In *Macbeth* the time period of Duncan's murder is framed first by the bell that is rung to bring Macbeth his wine and finally by the bell that clatters to alarm the castle, and so perhaps both Conrad and Hawthorne lifted their bell from Shakespeare.

Stevie's death has torn her personality "into two pieces, whose mental operations did not adjust themselves very well to each other." She had become cunning:

> Her right hand skimmed slightly the end of the table, and when she had passed on towards the sofa the carving knife had vanished without the slightest sound from the side of the dish. Mr. Verloc heard the creaky plank in the floor, and was content. He waited. Mrs. Verloc was coming.

But not to woo him!

> As if the homeless soul of Stevie had flown for shelter straight to the breast of his sister, guardian, and protector, the resemblance of her face with that of her brother grew at every step, even to the droop of the lower lip, even to the slight divergence of the eyes. But Mr. Verloc did not see that. He was lying on his back and staring upwards.

Conrad has shifted his camera from Winnie's to Adolf Verloc's point-of-view, and the effect of slow speech is created both by this shift in point-of-view and by the repetition of a motif which impedes the temporal progression. Here is a prose representation of slow time:

> He saw partly on the ceiling and partly on the wall the moving shadow of an arm with a clenched hand holding a carving knife. It flickered up and down. Its movements were leisurely. *They were leisurely enough* for Mr. Verloc to recognize the limb and the weapon.
> *They were leisurely enough* for him to take in the full meaning of the portent, and to taste the flavour of death rising in his gorge. His wife had

---

In both *Macbeth* and *The House of the Seven Gables* the bell transports us from the framed segment of time terminated, a hole in time's continuity and in the progression of narrated events; transports us back from this segment of time fixed and dead to life and time's flux. Verloc's shop-bell has the same symbolic import, but its symbolic import is not confined solely to this one. In *The Secret Agent* the shop-bell rings both before and after the murder, but the interim consumes such a time-span that only the chronologist would notice this bell-enclosing device.

As for other points of comparison, both Hawthorne and Conrad render the dead man as alive, *and* render the living as more dead than alive (with the exception of Holgrave and the scissor-grinder and Ned Higgins and Venner, etc.); in *Macbeth* the resurrected Banquo contends against the living Macbeth, and this ghost destroys his enjoyment of point-present nowness. The Pyncheons are similarly haunted by Maule's curse. All three works dramatize the theme of time.

Both Hawthorne and Conrad evince a predilection for circles. Concentric circles diagram the seven generations of Pyncheons, and circular selfhoods—patented by Hawthorne—reappear conspicuously in *The Secret Agent*. Another point of parallelism is the circular form of both novels. Again, both novels open on a cutback in the time-sequence, the opening action in both novels beginning in Chapter II.

gone raving mad—murdering mad. *They were leisurely enough* for the
first paralyzing effect of this discovery to pass away before a resolute
determination to come out victorious from the ghastly struggle with that
armed lunatic. *They were leisurely enough* for Mr. Verloc to elaborate a
plan of defence involving a dash behind the table, and the felling of the
woman to the ground with a heavy wooden chair. *But they were not
leisurely enough* to allow Mr. Verloc the time to move either hand or foot.
The knife was already planted in his breast. It met no resistance on its
way. Hazard has such accuracies (pp. 262–263).

Mr. Verloc's time-sense lags, and his theory of the situation is shattered
by the incalculable. Theory or Fixed Idea versus the Shock of the
Unpredictable—*that* patterns everything in the book.

Mrs. Verloc, in turn, is likewise confounded by a fixed idea. It's
the fixed idea that a murder stops the clock. Whereas it seems to her that
much time has elapsed since the moment of the murder, "As a matter of
fact, only three minutes had elapsed from the moment she had drawn
the first deep, easy breath after the blow, to this moment when Mrs.
Verloc formed the resolution to drown herself in the Thames. But Mrs.
Verloc could not believe that" (p. 269). The clock, *that too* has deceived her. A ticking sound breaks the silence of the room, but she
cannot believe that it could possibly come from the clock on the wall
because it doesn't fit her theory. Nevertheless,

> It grew upon her ear, while she remembered clearly that the clock on the
> wall was silent, had no audible tick. What did it mean by beginning to tick
> so loudly all of a sudden? . . . Mrs. Verloc cared nothing for time, and
> the ticking went on. She concluded it could not be the clock, and her
> sullen gaze moved along the walls, wavered, and became vague, while she
> strained her hearing to locate the sound. Tic, tic, tic.

Suddenly, what replaces the *ticking* of the seemingly stopped clock is
the trickling of blood from Verloc's corpse, the drops falling "fast and
furious like the pulse of an insane clock. At its highest speed this *ticking*
changed into a continuous sound of trickling." The Conradian pun
identifies clocks and blood, time and life.

As "Mr. Verloc was temperamentally no respecter of persons"
(XI), neither was he a respecter of conventions, nor of time and reality.
In his denial of Time-Now he shares with Winnie Verloc, who cared
nothing for time, and with Professor X, whose lifetime project is the
destruction of what *is*. And again, like Professor X, Verloc's resemblance "to a mechanical figure went so far that he had an automaton's

absurd air of being aware of the machinery inside him'' (IX). Verloc has no ideas, and his wife thinks only in images. So they are pretty much in accord, and especially so once Verloc is dead: "Except for the fact that Mrs. Verloc breathed these two would have been perfectly in accord: that accord of prudent reserve without superfluous words, and sparing of signs, which had been the foundation of their respectable home life'' (XI). Their domestic existence for seven years has been "stagnant and deep like a placid pool.'' In mourning for Stevie, Mrs. Verloc dresses in black and masks her face with a black veil: "all black—black as commonplace death itself, crowned with a few cheap and pale flowers.'' She personifies death veiled as life. When Ossipon discovers the bloody truth that Mrs. Verloc is a murderess, he is terrified. "He saw the woman twined round him like a snake, not to be shaken off. She was not deadly. She was death itself—the companion of life.'' At the end, all that remains of Winnie is her wedding ring. That "gold circlet of the wedding ring on Mrs. Verloc's left hand [had] glittered exceedingly with the untarnished glory of a piece from some splendid treasure of jewels, dropped in a dust-bin.''

When Winnie had fled the shop, what stopped her at the door was this memento of her late husband: "A round hat disclosed in the middle of the floor by the moving of the table rocked slightly on its crown in the wind of her flight'' (XI). Unnerved by that hat, she fails to turn out the light and she leaves the door ajar. Bewilderment and confusion occur again when Comrade Ossipon first sees the hat on his returning to the shop to put out the light and close the door. Now

> the true sense of the scene he was beholding came to Ossipon through the contemplation of the hat. It seemed an extraordinary thing, an ominous object, a sign. Black, and rim upward, it lay on the floor before the couch as if prepared to receive the contributions of pence from people who would come presently to behold Mr. Verloc in the fullness of his domestic ease reposing on a sofa. . . . Mr. Verloc did not seem so much asleep now as lying down with a bent head and looking insistently at his left breast. And when Comrade Ossipon had made out the handle of the knife he turned away from the glazed door, and retched violently (XII).

Ossipon "was not superstitious but there was too much blood on the floor; a beastly pool of it all round the hat.'' This blood-encircled hat upsets his theory that Verloc was the person who was blown to bits at Greenwich. Here's the hat, and there's Verloc sound asleep.

Even at dinner Verloc wore his round hat, and—hatted thus—he indicates his disrespect for conventions, social rituals, and the very feast of life. *That hat represents life misused or denied.* Thus Verloc disregarded "as usual the fate of his hat, which, as if accustomed to take care of itself, made for a safe shelter under the table" (XI). Having fished under the sofa for his *misplaced hat,* Verloc on finding it "held it *as if he did not know the use of a hat*" (IX). To Stevie, on the contrary, Verloc's hat was a sacred object because it belonged to his beloved mentor and savior. Stevie on one occasion pounced on that hat "and bore it off *reverently* into the kitchen." Whereupon Mrs. Verloc remarked: "You could do anything with that boy, Adolf. . . . He would go through fire for you" (IX). And he does just that. From the fireworks of the exploded bomb the only thing left to identify the disintegrated victim is a rag of a velvet collar with an address label on it—Stevie's sister had sewn it there as a precaution lest poor Stevie forget his home address. It is this label that traps Verloc.

> That his wife should hit upon the precaution of sewing the boy's address inside his overcoat was the last thing Mr. Verloc would have thought of. One can't think of everything. That was what she meant when she said that he need not worry if he lost Stevie during their walks. She had assured him that the boy would turn up all right. Well, he had turned up with a vengeance! (XI).

Chief Inspector Heat is bewildered by this unaccountable evidence—"I don't account for it at all, sir. It's simply unaccountable. It can't be explained by what I know" (VI). What's to be explained about that triangular label is that it is at once the emblem of Verloc's betrayal of humanity *and* the emblem of Winnie's fidelity, devotion, and love for a human being. Verloc has sacrificed an idiot for an idea, a human being for a theory, the concrete thing for the abstraction. Abstractions earned nothing but Conrad's scorn.

The triangle which identifies the anonymous Secret Agent Verloc—signifying both anonymity and insularity—links with the triangle of Brett Street where Verloc lives insulated from sunlight and from life itself. Triangles and circles in *The Secret Agent* have multiple significances. Now there is nothing unpredictable about Mr. Verloc, theoretically speaking from Chief Inspector Heat's point of view, and yet the triangular sign of Verloc's identity becomes—in the triangle of the coat label—*the emblem of the unpredictableness of things.* Again, betrayal and fidelity are written there—the whole moral meaning of the novel. Only Winnie would have thought of that label, out of love for her brother. And he alone, that half-wit, believed in Verloc—believed in man. How irrational can man get?

III

When Stevie is confused he draws circles, and when Winnie is confused she remembers Stevie drawing circles: "Mrs. Verloc was sitting in the place where poor Stevie usually established himself of an evening with paper and pencil for the pastime of drawing these coruscations of innumerable circles suggesting chaos and eternity" (XI). When Stevie drew circles it was while sitting beside a clock. By drawing circles Stevie found sanctuary from time and from the revolutionists' theories of violence against time. He found sanctuary against chaos and confusion in the form manifested by a circle. What Stevie designed, however, represents both form and its opposite, chaos and confusion: "a coruscating whirl of circles that by their tangled multitude of repeated curves, uniformity of form and confusion of intersecting lines suggested a rendering of cosmic chaos, the symbolism of a mad art attempting the inconceivable" (III). What is inconceivable is eternity. "But eternity," as Comrade Ossipon envisions it, "is a damned hole" (XIII). A circle, itself the sign of perfection of form, represents thus a hole in time's continuity—time confused and chaotic, disarranged, terminated (as signified by the blood-encircled hat), or suspended (as signified in the murder scene when clock-time seemingly stops). Circles and their emblematic objects associate with conditions or states of mental confusion because they represent the impingement of the unexpected thing, symbolizing Time the Unpredictable. That is what Time, as distinguished from calculable clock-time, *is*. It is a hole in time's continuity, the unpredictable event in routine clocked existence. Hence, a circle represents insularity from time or life itself. Conrad's example is Verloc's blood-encircled round hat. Eternity's a damned hole. What eternity lacks is precisely what characterizes life or time's continuity, namely the unpredictableness of things. As Razumov in *Under Western Eyes* leaves Haldin's rooms he becomes a figure in "eternity"—with his watch broken, time stands still. When Stevie draws circles, holes in time. he is "very good and quiet," and when Razumov attempts to define Eternity, the inconceivable, he defines it as "something dull and quiet. There would be nothing unexpected—don't you see? The element of time would be wanting" (I). Obsessed with his theories and fixed ideas, Chief Inspector Heat is not very wise, since true wisdom "is not certain of anything *in this world of contradictions*. . . . His wisdom was of an official kind, or else he might have reflected upon a matter not of theory but of experience that in the close-woven stuff of relations between conspirator and police there occur unexpected solutions of continuity, *sudden holes in space and time*" (V).

The time bomb—comprised of Chemical X and concocted by Professor X—is unexpectedly exploded by X, the unknown and incalculable factor in Verloc's calculated plot, in Vladimir's theory of bomb-throwing, and in Chief Inspector Heat's fixed idea. "Impossible!" exclaims Heat on first learning of the explosion. What is deadly to fixed ideas is X, the unknown thing. The example is the root of a tree stump on which Stevie stumbled, blowing himself into eternity. In that unexpected obstacle of a tree stump Nature asserts its supremacy against man's conspiracy to destroy what *is*. The attack on the first meridian represents anarchy against Time, blasphemy against God and Nature.

Whereas Vladimir's theory aims at the destruction of science, Professor X's theory aims at the destruction of conventions by which mankind is restrained. Exterminate the multitude—the weak, the flabby, the silly, the cowardly, the faint of heart, and the slavish of mind. "Theirs is the kingdom of the earth. Exterminate! Exterminate! That is the only way of progress. . . . Every taint, every vice, every prejudice, every convention meets its doom" (XIII). "To destroy public faith in legality was the imperfect formula of his pedantic fanaticism. . . . He was a moral agent—that was settled in his mind" (V). In fact, however, the only true moral agent is Time. The Patroness, on temperamental grounds, "defies time with a scornful disregard, as if it were a rather vulgar convention submitted to by the mass of inferior mankind." Chief Inspector Heat, contemplating the instantaneous death of the victim of the explosion, rises momentarily "above the vulgar conception of time." "Instantaneous! He remembered all he had ever read in popular publications of long and terrifying dreams dreamed in the instant of waking; of the whole of past life lived with frightful intensity by a drowning man as his doomed head bobs up . . . for the last time." Heat experiences an epiphany—he envisions ages of atrocious pain and mental torture as being contained "between two successive winks of an eye" (V). Verloc's eyes, because they are "not well adapted to winking," perceive nothing of life in the Moment-Now —Time-Now happens between two successive winks. The Privy Councillor of the Russian Embassy, Wurmt, is literally shortsighted, and in the second sense of the word the Revolutionists of the Future are also shortsighted.

It is not until Mrs. Verloc confronts the clock after the murder that, for the first occasion in her life, she is made aware of time. It is not until Verloc is dead that he is rendered as though he were alive, for then, as he lies murdered on the sofa and Ossipon leaves the shop, the cracked bell clatters "as if trying in vain to warn the reposing Mr. Verloc of the final departure of his wife—accompanied by his friend" (XII). To perfect a detonator adjustable "to all conditions of action, and even to unexpected changes of conditions," Professor X needs more time. Exterminate Universal Time: "what's wanted is a clean sweep and a clear start for a new conception of life." "But the time! the time! Give me time! Ah! that multitude too stupid to feel either pity or fear. Sometimes I think they have everything on their side. Everything—even death —my own weapon." Blow-me-to-bits Professor X (he is death "enlisted in the service of humanity") rebukes Chief Inspector Heat, who personifies the convention of life: "I am doing my work better than you're doing yours." Much better, no doubt of that, since Professor X is, to identify him, Death—the human representation of deadly time. Agent of Death, and therefore, "I shall never be arrested." He is a parody of Time the Unpredictable. Insofar as he is human he is also imperfect, for no man can convert himself into a perfect automaton no matter how much machinery he carries inside himself. In the explosion at Maze Hill Station an unpredicted event confounds the calculated one—Stevie is blown to bits, instead of the first meridian. The imperfect bomb detonates—symbolically—at the wall protecting Greenwich Observatory, appropriately at Maze Hill.

Theories—scientific, political, sociological, economic, psychological—all are reduced to zero by Conrad's diabolic irony. What protection against life that we devise consists of superstitions, myths, theories, conventional conceptions of reality, systems and creeds, codes of behavior by which society is manipulated and controlled; in sum, all that the muddling intellect contrives. The nihilism of *The Secret Agent* ends in a covert affirmation of the supremacy of life. Could we but manipulate reality so that what happens happens as predicted, but no! Time-Now is the Unpredictable, life in all its irrational particulars; including *X* the unknown event. Wherefore I conclude that it is Time the Unpredictable—agent of life and death—that Conrad's novel cryptographically intends as *the* Secret Agent.[7]

---

[7] For further readings of *The Secret Agent* since my "Time and *The Secret Agent*" appeared in *Texas Studies in Literature and Language* I (1):101–122 (1959), see my "Studies of Conrad's *The Secret Agent* Since 1960," *Conradiana* VI (2) (Summer 1974).

  This survey essay draws upon my "Checklist of Some Studies of Conrad's *The Secret Agent* Since 1960," *Conradiana* VI (1):31–45 (Spring 1974).

Albert Guerard

Two Versions of Anarchy: Under Western Eyes

Under Western Eyes [unlike *The Secret Agent*], however, is a great tragic novel. It is Conrad's final and in some ways most moving treatment of his central story of betrayal and self-punishment. The terms of "The Secret Sharer" are now reversed. The Razumov who chooses to protect society and who betrays the outlaw brother and double Victor Haldin has betrayed himself first of all. But it is rather with *Lord Jim* that *Under Western Eyes* demands to be examined, if only because the two novels are more comparable in length and density. Once again we have the story of a not uncommon man whom chance and suffering render extraordinary; who suddenly has to face a boundary-situation and most difficult choice; whose crime both makes and breaks him. The act of betrayal, carrying him out of one solitude and into another, lends him a somber magnitude and new moral awareness, and compels him to destroy himself at last. Responses will vary among different readers and different generations as to which act of betrayal was the more fundamental, Razumov's or Lord Jim's. (In the early 1950's, in America, neither the informing on Haldin nor the employment as a police spy would have seemed anything but commendable to certain readers.) But the plot of *Under Western Eyes* builds more impressively than *Lord Jim*'s, after the betrayal occurs, and offers a less equivocal pattern of redemption. *Under Western Eyes* never threatens to descend into popular adventure and romance, as *Lord Jim* occasionally does.

Why then does it occupy a slightly less commanding position in the Conrad canon? Presumably because it is distinctly the less original novel of the two. The study of Razumov's guilt and of the Russian temperament generally cannot fail to remind us of Dostoevsky, though Conrad's is a different and far more orderly manner. And there is a much less impressive dramatization of certain psychological processes than in *Lord Jim*. The art of *Under Western Eyes,* moreover—its manipulation of the reader through structure and texture, plot and reflexive reference—is more conventional. It does not to the same degree stand between the reader and the material to control that reader's response. *Under Western Eyes* is Conrad's best realistic novel. But it is not an "art novel" of infinite complexity, and it does not, like *Lord Jim,* change and greatly expand on second and subsequent readings.

Razumov in himself (considered, that is, apart from the narrator's musings on him) is psychologically a fuller and more important creation than Lord Jim. Or, at least, he is a more interesting person. The initial betrayal and the half-conscious stages leading to it are dramatized with great subtlety and economy. For the decision to inform on Haldin is no sudden accident of failing will or swift forestalling vision. At the outset Razumov is "as lonely in the world as a man swimming in the deep sea." He has seen his father Prince K—— once. Once too he saw his half-sisters descend from a carriage, and "felt a glow of warm friendliness towards these girls who would never know of his existence." For he has only the "immense parentage" of Russia, and no more intimate conscious longing than for the silver medal offered by the Ministry of Education for a prize essay. He combines, rather curiously for Conrad, the vulnerable solitary and the sane hard worker. "Razumov was one of those men who, living in a period of mental and political unrest, keep an instinctive hold on normal, practical, everyday life. He was aware of the emotional tension of his time; he even responded to it in an indefinite way. But his main concern was with his work, his studies, and with his own future." Some day, perhaps, he will be a "celebrated old professor."

This is the unawakened man. His stable existence is shattered in the worst possible way when Haldin appears in his room to acknowledge the assassination and ask for help. "The sentiment of his life being utterly ruined by this contact with such a crime expressed itself quaintly by a sort of half-derisive mental exclamation, 'There goes my silver medal!' " He is all the more indignant when Haldin tells him one of the reasons why he was chosen for this confidence: he had no family to suffer in the event his complicity came out. "Because I haven't that, must everything else be taken away from me?" Yet he sets out on his errand of mercy to find the driver Ziemianitch, impelled by instinctive loyalty to a fellow student and perhaps even by his "personal longings of liberalism." The account of his approach to political conversion on that night is brief but extremely convincing: his egoism and fear create the doctrinal commitment which alone can rationalize the betrayal. Thus the inert drunken Ziemianitch, whom he beats in frustrated rage, provokes meditations on power and the "stern hand." And Razumov's personal plight ("done for" between "the drunkenness of the peasant incapable of action and the dream-intoxication of the idealist incapable of perceiving the reason of things") is by implication national.

At this point, "conscious now of a tranquil, unquenchable hate," he has his first phantom vision of Haldin lying on his bed as if dead. The half-conscious mind at least is approaching that decision to betray. "Must one kill oneself to escape this visitation?" In rage he stamps his foot on the snow, and under it feels the "hard ground of Russia, inanimate, cold, inert, like a sullen and tragic mother hiding her face under a winding-sheet." He experiences an intuition of Russia's "sacred inertia," which must not be touched, and of absolute power which must be preserved for the great autocrat of the future. Within, some "superior power had inspired him with a flow of masterly argument." The superior power is his ability to rationalize and generalize selfish aims. It interweaves, indeed masterfully, his concern with his possibly ruined career and his awareness of Haldin as a disruptive political force; his selfish rage and his theory of the throne. He is disturbed in his reflections by the yell of one sledgedriver to another, "Oh, thou vile wretch!" But the phrase drives him on rather than deters him. Immediately afterward he experiences his hallucination of Haldin lying in the snow across his path. He forces himself to walk over the breast of the phantom—and decides to give Haldin up. Betray him? "All a man can betray is his conscience. And how is my conscience engaged here; by what bond of common faith, of common conviction, am I obliged to let that fanatical idiot drag me down with him?" His decision, as the narrator remarks, "could hardly be called a decision. He had simply discovered what he had meant to do all along." And when the long evening is ending (after he has informed on Haldin, after Haldin has left his room) he hears himself say "I confess"; and thinks of himself as on a rack. This is, surely, great dramatic writing. But the drama is largely within.

For the remainder of the novel Razumov is always on a rack; or on the two racks of fear and guilt. There are times when it is difficult to distinguish between the two, and if the analysis of guilt is more impressive, the dramatization of fear is more exciting. The greatest actual menace is a Dostoevskian *dédoublement* and consequent reckless volubility and snarling uneasiness. Razumov watches appalled his own indiscretions and temptations to confess. Even before Haldin is arrested, he speaks to General T—— with dangerous violence. The rack turns after the police visit to his room and more swiftly through the interview with Councillor Mikulin. Even as he talks Razumov is appalled by his own flow of hasty words, and during the interview has a frightening vision of "his own brain suffering on the rack—a long, pale figure drawn asunder horizontally with terrific force. . . ." And when he becomes a police spy (having found no other answer to Councillor Mikulin's sinister question "Where to?") the real danger is immeasurably increased.

In Geneva he is unwisely talkative with Peter Ivanovitch and with Sophia Antonovna, who had been sent to Geneva to verify an identity. He stupidly insists on the distrust of the exiles, but he had largely invented that distrust; he is aware of his savage curtness and cannot control it. "Even as he spoke he reproached himself for his words, for his tone. All day long he had been saying the wrong things. It was folly, worse than folly. It was weakness; it was this disease of perversity overcoming his will." From the first moment he behaves unwisely in front of the killer Necator, who will presently burst his eardrums. In the grand traditional pattern Razumov, literally menaced by death, is throughout his own worst enemy. When he has finally won outward impunity he must, because of that other rack of guilt, confess what no one would have ever discovered.

The two racks turn in unison. It would be hard to conceive a plot more successfully combining dramatic suspense and psycho-moral significance. Through the second and much of the third part the reader has no certain knowledge that Razumov, welcomed in Geneva as the late Haldin's friend and associate, is actually a police spy. The motives for his presence might as plausibly be inward ones: a self-destructive tempting of fate; a compulsion to confront those most likely to destroy him; even, an unconscious effort to appease guilt through reenactment of the crime. "Ah, Peter Ivanovitch, if you only knew the force which drew—no, which *drove* me towards you! The irresistible force." Razumov is thinking of Councillor Mikulin. But the reader is likely to think of a generalized self-destructiveness, and the reader not Razumov would be right. That *is* the hidden motive, hidden even from him. Thus Razumov, in his "satanic" game of suggesting yet concealing a second and truer meaning from Peter Ivanovitch, stumbles with unconscious irony upon a third and truest one. Only he can do the "work" of redeeming himself through confession; he has indeed been impelled, by the strongest of psychic drives; he does not stand before Ivanovitch confessed, but someday he will. And a "blind tool" he may well be, though at the end he will go as far as possible toward converting compulsion into moral choice. But Razumov, of course, has no idea he is saying all this:

You have been condescending enough. I quite understood it was to lead me on. You must render me the justice that I have not tried to please. I have been impelled, compelled, or rather sent—let us say sent—towards you for a work that no one but myself can do. You would call it a harmless delusion: a ridiculous delusion at which you don't even smile. It is absurd of me to talk like this, yet some day you will remember these words, I hope. Enough of this. Here I stand before you—confessed! But one thing more I must add to complete it: a mere blind tool I can never consent to be.[1]

By delaying as long as he does the formal revelation that Razumov is Mikulin's agent, Conrad preserves a sympathy that would (with a more abrupt procedure) have been lost. We must see Razumov suffer before we see, nakedly, this second of his crimes. And the "deceptive" impression that Razumov is obeying a psycho-moral compulsion is not deceptive at all. He has been sent to Geneva to write incriminating reports on the exiles. He will write instead his diary and condemning self-analysis.

The novel's anatomy of guilt is Dostoevskian, which means that it is true; the difference is that Conrad's method is infinitely more selective. His dramatization of the phantom, for instance, and its slow attenuation from sharp hallucination to symbolic force and allusion, is remarkably tactful and convincing. The original vision on the snow (coinciding with the decision to give Haldin up) is reported in a cool, matter-of-fact prose. It is a "phenomenon," and Razumov tackles it calmly. But when he reaches his room, and finds Haldin lying on his bed as though already dead, he reflects: "I have walked over his chest." He touches Haldin's shoulder and at once feels "an insane temptation to grip that exposed throat and squeeze the breath out of that body, lest it should escape his custody, leaving only a phantom behind." The vision during the Mikulin interview of his own brain suffering on the rack is also of this Haldin-phantom. And shortly after that interview (as we glance ahead to Part IV) Razumov sees Haldin as a "moral spectre infinitely more effective than any visible apparition of the dead." He thinks that the specter cannot haunt his own room, through which the living Haldin had blundered; supposes, glancing at the bed, that he would never actually see anything there. But only two pages later he does.

Through much of the second and even third parts we have little chance to see the phantom, since we long watch Razumov from the outside. But we note his stammering "compelled" remarks to Madame de S—— that he too had had an "experience," had once seen a phantom. The interview with Sophia Antonovna, treated more subjectively,

[1]*Under Western Eyes,* pp. 228–229.

shows that the phantom has become featureless; is becoming, so to speak, a component of mental discourse. "He had argued himself into new beliefs; and he had made for himself a mental atmosphere of gloomy and sardonic reverie, a sort of murky medium through which the event appeared like a featureless shadow having vaguely the shape of a man; a shape extremely familiar, yet utterly inexpressive, except for its air of discreet waiting in the dusk." Razumov thinks of it as "not alarming." But this quiet prose certainly conveys alarm, and on the next page his allusions to Madame de S——'s spiritualist powers and to the "cold ghost" of a tea seem mildly obsessive. The phantom, which had been "left behind lying powerless and passive on the pavement covered with snow," is perhaps most powerful when embodied in Mrs. Haldin and Nathalie on the long night of confessions. "The fifteen minutes with Mrs. Haldin were like the revenge of the unknown." There is something Razumov cannot understand in her manner; she is as white as a ghost; she falls into an incomprehensible silence. But the terms are naturalistic; Haldin continued to exist, but "in the affection of that mourning old woman." Razumov strides from the room, leaving her behind; it is "frankly a flight." But he comes upon Nathalie. "Her presence in the ante-room was as unforseen as the appearance of her brother had been." And the time for a full confession has come.

The phantom (whether as hallucination, psychic symbol, or short-hand notation of anxiety) does not have the major part in the story of Razumov's torment. The ferocious ironies of his situation, rather, con-stitute that major part: to be honored by his fellow-students for a sup-posed complicity in the assassination; honored by Haldin himself for his "unstained, lofty, and solitary" existence; welcomed by the Geneva exiles with respect and by Nathalie Haldin with a dedicated passion, and who has, thanks to the betrayal, the only real conversation with his father in his whole life. Razumov's immediate response (waking chilled on the morning after Haldin's capture) is not fear or shame but a plausi-ble mental stagnation and inertia. His "conservative convictions . . . had become crystallized by the shock of his contact with Hal-din." However, his notes and books have become a "mere litter of blackened paper." He compels himself to go to the library, but an "in-finite distress . . . annihilated his energy." The apathetic state passes, after the interview with Councillor Mikulin, into an actual psychosomat-ic illness, briefly and brilliantly described.[2] He emerges from it to find things "subtly and provokingly" changed. But he continues to suffer from ennui, the fitfulness and dread when outside alternating with a

[2]*Ibid.*, p. 298.

total inertia when at home. One might suppose the room would become ''morally uninhabitable.'' But this does not happen, perhaps because Razumov has now entered into his second and testing solitude:

> On the contrary, he liked his lodgings better than any other shelter he, who had never known a home, had ever hired before. He liked his lodgings so well that often, on that very account, he found a certain difficulty in making up his mind to go out. It resembled a physical seduction such as, for instance, makes a man reluctant to leave the neighborhood of a fire on a cold day.[3]

The portrait is psychologically and dramatically true. But it cannot be conveyed through summary, nor reduced to the shortcuts of psychological discourse. The very great scene of Razumov's confession to Nathalie Haldin cannot (though we recognize such elements as the phantom) be abstracted at all. The scene is as it were irreducible. Even the furnishings of the little anteroom, with its remorseless light and its hooks recalling the hook on which Ziemianitch was found hanging, seem part of the inward experience. The drama is intensified by the unconscious irony of the teacher of languages, who thinks he is to witness a love scene: ''The period of reserve was over; he was coming forward in his own way.'' Razumov is indeed coming forward; but ''watching himself inwardly, as though he were trying to count his own heart-beats, while his eyes never for a moment left the face of the girl.'' He exists, speaks under the greatest conceivable strain. For this is now a matter of life and death, of moral life or death. The great spectacle is of the mind breaking willfully not compulsively through its long habit of evasion, calculating its moves, pausing long enough to ask about the efficacy of remorse; and circling down to the truth. The denunciation of self does not involve a blind jump from one state of being to another. The final speeches, on the contrary, bring into play and as it were into the open all the essentials of Razumov's being, and all the terms of his conflict. His triumph is a genuine one.

For the crime which had broken Razumov has now fully made him. Thus he has the strength necessary, after leaving Nathalie Haldin, to add certain confessions to his diary and then go before the assembled revolutionists at the house of Julius Laspara, there to put his back against the wall and make his public confession. ''He was the puppet of his past,'' yet also a free agent to some degree. The comment made later by Sophia Antonovna applies well enough to both confessions:

[3]*Ibid.,* p. 299.

Well, call it what you like; but tell me, how many of them would deliver themselves up deliberately to perdition (as he himself says in that book) rather than go on living, secretly debased in their own eyes? How many? . . . And please mark this—he was safe when he did it. It was just when he believed himself safe and more—infinitely more—when the possibility of being loved by that admirable girl first dawned upon him, that he discovered that his bitterest railings, the worst wickedness, the devil work of his hate and pride, could never cover up the ignominy of the existence before him. There's character in such a discovery.[4]

The written confession (pp. 358–362) raises the one serious question concerning the characterization's over-all authenticity and firmness. For the Razumov of these pages, whose voice and style are fairly convincing, claims to have been a much more cynical person, in his relationship with Nathalie Haldin, than we have had any reason to suspect. A few sentences (which I draw together from two pages of the novel and which therefore falsify their texture and pace) will indicate how very much is claimed:

I was given up to evil. I exulted in having induced that silly innocent fool to steal his father's money. He was a fool, but not a thief. I made him one. It was necessary. I had to confirm myself in my contempt and hate for what I betrayed . . . Listen—now comes the true confession. The other was nothing. To save me, your trustful eyes had to entice my thought to the very edge of the blackest treachery. . . . And do you know what I said to myself? I shall steal his sister's soul from her. When we met that first morning in the gardens, and you spoke to me confidingly in the generosity of your spirit, I was thinking, 'Yes, he himself by talking of her trustful eyes has delivered her into my hands!' If you could have looked then into my heart, you would have cried out aloud with terror and disgust. . . . Perhaps no one will believe the baseness of such an intention to be possible . . . every word of that friend of yours was egging me on to the unpardonable sin of stealing a soul. . . . I returned to look at you every day, and drink in your presence the poison of my infamous intention.[5]

The conception is a powerful one: Dostoevskian if not Russian, perhaps simply human. Moreover, it is at least logically consonant with a psychology which sees in reënactment one of the spirit's few ways of coping with unappeased guilt. One function of the phantom is to remind us, and Razumov, that Haldin must be killed again and again. And the conception appears plausible enough if we go outside the novel to speculate on the possibilities for evil of a man who has done what

[4]*Ibid.*, p. 380.
[5]*Ibid.*, pp. 359–360.

Razumov has already done. And yet it seems (coming so late in the story) rhetorical, arbitrary, untrue. One reason may be that symbolic reënactments are rarely as conscious as this. A more important reason is that we have known Razumov only as a man on the two racks of fear and guilt. He has had little time for anything else. But most of all, the claims seem untrue to everything we have seen of his relationship with Nathalie Haldin.

The very first meeting was a brief one. But her first remarks to Razumov—"You are Mr. Razumov." . . . "Can't you guess who I am?" . . . "Victor—Victor Haldin!"—are enough to send him reeling against the wall of the terrace. (Later, Razumov is "tempted to flight at the mere recollection" of that meeting.) His response to the first interview in the narrator's presence is a curious irritability and an "unrefreshed, motionless stare, the stare of a man who lies unwinking in the dark, angrily passive in the toils of disastrous thoughts." There is no reason to believe, here, that the "disastrous thoughts" are other than those prompted by fear and guilt. Furthermore, not all our view of Razumov's relationship with Nathalie Haldin is from the outside. Whatever intentions he had to "steal the soul" would surely have come out on the occasion of Peter Ivanovitch's request that he, *la personne indiquée,* bring Nathalie to the Chateau Borel group. Tekla explains to him, a few minutes later, why such a contact would be ruinously disillusioning for her. The occasion for evil is thus propitious. But Razumov's inward reaction is a vague one of *dédoublement,* loathing, uneasiness.

Was the diabolism confessed in writing then only an afterthought, a new idea discovered this late in the novel and too attractive to expunge? The more probable explanation is that Conrad, writing here in Razumov's name for the first time, returned imaginatively to his original plan for the novel. It was to have been entitled *Razumov,* and would have involved much more melodrama. And it would have dramatized a much greater cynicism:

> 2d in Genève. The student Razumov meeting abroad the mother and sister of Haldin falls in love with that last, marries her and, after a time, confesses to her the part he played in the arrest of her brother.
>
> The psychological developments leading to Razumov's betrayal of Haldin, to the confession of the fact to his wife and to the death of these people (brought about mainly by the resemblance of their child to the late Haldin), form the real subject of the story.[6]

The temptation to steal the soul may be described as another "lost subject."

[6]Letter to John Galsworthy, January 6, 1908. *Life and Letters,* II, p. 65.

Otherwise, the characterization of Razumov is altogether impressive. It would be futile to try to define with exactness the creative situation behind it. There are depths below depths in these matters, and a symbolic repudiation of self may turn out to be, finally, a secret justification. But the situation was certainly an intense one, involving no small degree of intellectual identification with Razumov, informer and police spy. It is as though an officer sharing far more of Conrad's convictions than Jim had leaped off the *Patna*. The author recognizes the egoistic sources of Razumov's conversion, and he does not share the mystical absolutism of his new faith. But he lends to Razumov the very language of his own scorn of visionaries, even the favorite and personal *secular:* "Visionaries work everlasting evil on earth. Their Utopias inspire in the mass of mediocre minds a disgust of reality and a contempt for the secular logic of human development." He would agree with Razumov that "twenty thousand bladders inflated by the noblest sentiments and jostling against each other in the air are a miserable incumbrance of space, holding no power, possessing no will, having nothing to give."

Thus the reasoned political credo Razumov writes immediately after Haldin's arrest could serve as Conrad's own:

> History not Theory.
> Patriotism not Internationalism.
> Evolution not Revolution.
> Direction not Destruction.
> Unity not Disruption.[7]

The student Razumov at the outset shows, moreover (and in the Author's Note as well as in the text), the supreme maritime virtues of sanity and steadiness. Even the betrayal of Haldin, seen in the context of Conrad's respect for law and distrust of revolution, could be said to correspond with certain authorial convictions.

But only with convictions, and only with certain of these. The energizing conflict derives from the fact that Razumov, this sane conservative scorner of visionaries and servant of law and victim of revolutionary folly, is (when he informs on Haldin) dramatized as committing a crime; he has violated the deepest human bond. This implication seems to me unarguable. If it were not present, the rest of the novel would be morally meaningless. And it is of course the suffering guilty man (rather than the "ordinary young man" with "sane ambitions" of the Author's Note) who elicits the prolonged act of novelistic sympathy. "You have either to rot or to burn," Sophia Antonovna remarks in a

[7]*Under Western Eyes*, p. 66.

different context. The Razumov of the opening pages (whose "main concern was with his work, his studies, and with his own future") rots. He has not yet entered the moral universe, and he enters it by committing the crime. But thereafter he elicits as much sympathy (not approval) as any of Conrad's protagonists. The achievement of this dramatic sympathy is all the more remarkable, of course, because Razumov is not just any betrayer of the human bond. He is also a Russian.

"The most terrifying reflection (I am speaking now for myself) is that all these people are not the product of the exceptional but of the general—of the normality of their place, and time, and race. . . . The oppressors and the oppressed are all Russians together; and the world is brought once more face to face with the truth of the saying that the tiger cannot change his stripes nor the leopard his spots." Thus Conrad wrote of his characters years afterward, and three years after the Revolution, in his Author's Note. But the novel itself shows no little ambivalence, and perhaps its greatest act of imaginative integrity (i.e., fidelity to such truth as the dream discovers) is its marked creative sympathy with Russia and Russians, a sympathy which extends even to some of the revolutionary exiles. "I think that I am trying to capture the very soul of things Russian," Conrad wrote to Galsworthy. But he was at least briefly captured by that soul, and on the devil's side without knowing it. The narrator, to be sure, makes certain negative statements which Conrad would have signed in an essay or preface: on the spirit of Russia as the spirit of cynicism; on Russian scorn of the practical forms of political liberty; on her "terrible corroding simplicity in which mystic phrases clothe a naïve and hopeless cynicism"; on her detestation of life, "the irremediable life of the earth as it is. . . ."[8] But the novel's over-all tone is compassionate, and especially toward the sufferings reported by Tekla and Sophia Antonovna.

"Sometimes I think that it is only in Russia that there are such people and such a depth of misery can be reached." There runs throughout a counterpoint of East and West, which is in part a counterpoint of the suffering and the secure. "It is a very miserable and a very false thing to belong to the majority," Nathalie Haldin says, and the narrator pleads in defense of England's "bargain with fate" that she too has had tragic times. The contrast, if not between those who burn and those who rot, is between those who burn and those who have escaped from the fire. The teacher-narrator (at times much less sympathetic to Russia than is the novel as a whole) once seems almost to speak for its own uneasy conscience: "It is not for us, the staid lovers calmed by the possession of a conquered liberty, to condemn without appeal the

[8]*Ibid.*, pp. 67, 104.

fierceness of thwarted desire.'' Russia exists, to borrow Rathenau's famous phrase, in the soul-saving ''abyss of sin and suffering.''

The counterpoint becomes necessarily, and perhaps unluckily for the West, a counterpoint of Russia and Switzerland. And in the area of cool judgment there can be little doubt as to Conrad's preferences. They are for the order and stability of Swiss democratic institutions, as for the stolid decency of the English narrator. But Geneva is the ''respectable and passionless abode of democratic liberty,'' and the narrator himself composes a very tendentious contrast whose sympathies go in an entirely different direction. He considers the Bastions, where Nathalie Haldin and Razumov will meet:

> I saw these two, escaped out of four score of millions of human beings ground between the upper and nether millstone, walking under these trees, their young heads close together. Yes, an excellent place to stroll and talk in. It even occurred to me, while we turned once more away from the wide iron gates, that when tired they would have plenty of accommodation to rest themselves. There was a quantity of tables and chairs displayed between the restaurant chalet and the bandstand, a whole raft of painted deals spread out under the trees. In the very middle of it I observed a solitary Swiss couple, whose fate was made secure from the cradle to the grave by the perfected mechanism of democratic institutions in a republic that could almost be held by the palm of one's hand. The man, colourlessly uncouth, was drinking beer out of a glittering glass; the woman, rustic and placid, leaning back in the rough chair, gazed idly around.[9]

The counterpoint of Swiss and Russian would seem to be, as we consider all the references to Geneva and consider all of the narrator's complacencies, not merely one of the secure and the suffering, but also of the respectable and the anarchic, the decent and the messy, the complacent and the compassionate, the mercenary and the mystical, the ''saved'' and the tragic, the abstract and the human. The narrator's own obtuseness is one of the great sources of this created sympathy for the damned. His mumbling about ''Western readers'' and about ''a lurid, Russian colouring'' at the moment of the Haldins' most intense grief increases sympathy for the Russians generally. And his astonishment because the revolutionists visit the deafened Razumov throws an unfavorable light on his own automatic moralism, and a final light on their unexpected compassion.

Irving Howe's argument that the novel is weakened because it develops too little sympathy for the revolutionaries strikes me, in fact,

[9]*Ibid.*, p. 175.

as seriously mistaken.[10] It would be unreasonable to demand much for the squeaky-voiced killer Necator (himself a police spy, as it turns out) or for Julius Laspara. But Tekla in her appointed role as nurse and companion of the punished sinners (she herself recruited by a "saintly apple-woman") is a familiar Dostoevskian figure of compassion. Her narrative to Nathalie Haldin (pp. 149–155) is a moving account of suffering "inside Russia." It subtly prepares us, moreover, for Razumov's own fate, and on a second reading functions as very striking reflexive reference. (Her humble offer of her services to Razumov reveals an ear for feminine speech and feminine logic—or, it may be, a compassionate imagination rather than ear—not evident in the earlier novels.) And even the "wrong headed" Sophia Antonovna, as Conrad calls her in his Author's Note, wins some of the affection he normally accords durable old soldiers. For this is what she is: the white-haired veteran of revolution who had begun going to the secret societies at sixteen, and who had cut her hair as a "first step towards crushing the social infamy."

A novelistic sympathy for these women is natural enough. But there may also exist, in addition to such sympathy and in addition to a normal unconscious sympathy with the outlaw, a creative sympathy with the exceptional buffoon or exceptional object of contempt. Such may be the truest meaning of Milton's alliance with Satan, or of Shakespeare's with Iago and Richard III. And Dostoevsky's power to dramatize the fool as from within, many fools in fact, is one of the sure tokens of his genius. There is some of this in Conrad. He groups the feminist Peter Ivanovitch and Madame de S—— as "fair game" in his Author's Note. "They are the apes of a sinister jungle and are treated as their grimaces deserve." But the ironic account of Peter Ivanovitch's absurd heroic progress across Siberia, engirdled by his chain ("that simple engine of government") is one of the summits in Conrad's work.

It has a quality of vividness, humor, and phrasing that only imaginative sympathy can achieve. Mere scorn could not conceive the disastrous dropping of the file, or the faint jingling of the chain, or the "naked tawny figure glimpsed vaguely through the bushes with a cloud of mosquitoes and flies hovering about the shaggy head," or the leaves and twigs in his tangled hair that astonish his rescuer. Indeed mere scorn could hardly dramatize so well a fatuousness which describes the events leading up to his obtaining of the file as an "obscure episode . . . in the history of ideas in Russia." The retrospective narrative and image of Ivanovitch and his cloud of mosquitoes notably affects our present view

[10]"Joseph Conrad: Order and Anarchy: The Political Novels," *Kenyon Review* (Autumn 1953), pp. 505–521.

of him riding in a landau with Madame de S—— in Geneva: "the 'heroic fugitive' . . . sitting, portentously bearded and darkly bespec- tacled, not by her side, but opposite her, with his back to the horses. Thus, facing each other, with no one else in the roomy carriage, their airings suggested a conscious public manifestation." We may borrow the word. It may be that the imaginative sympathy (combined of course with the deepest scorn) is for Ivanovitch as a total, realized manifesta- tion of a type.

Cosas de Russia . . . This novel, if we are to believe either the classics of Russian fiction or the enigmatic accounts of current events, does come remarkably close to the "very soul of things Russian." The brief glimpses of life in St. Petersburg are most convincing. So too are Victor Haldin, with his strange speech on the "divine" resignation of the Russian soul; and the long bony student living on the fringe of conspiracy, and the contradictions of "Madcap" Kostia; and the fanatic General T——, and the weary Prince K—— with his aura of Western culture. Nathalie's vision of unity and her contempt for political parties are Russian; so too is her mystical vision of a time of concord. "Listen, Kirylo Sidorovitch. I believe that the future will be merciful to us all. Revolutionist and reactionary, victim and executioner, betrayer and betrayed, they shall all be pitied together when the light breaks on our black sky at last." Will Russians in their "land of spectral ideas and disembodied aspirations" turn always to autocracy and turn "at last from the vain and endless conflict to the one great historical fact of the land"? In any event the trial of Councillor Mikulin reminds us that much that has seemed grotesque in the Soviet system is, simply, Rus- sian:

> Later on the larger world first heard of him in the very hour of his downfall, during one of those State trials which astonish and puzzle the average plain man who reads the newspapers, by a glimpse of unsuspected intrigues. And in the stir of vaguely seen monstrosities, in that momen- tary, mysterious disturbance of muddy waters, Councillor Mikulin went under dignified, with only a calm, emphatic protest of his innocence —nothing more. No disclosures damaging to a harassed autocracy, com- plete fidelity to the secrets of the miserable *arcana imperii* deposited in his patriotic breast, a display of bureaucratic stoicism in a Russian official's ineradicable, almost sublime contempt for truth; stoicism of silence under- stood only by the very few of the initiated, and not without a certain cynical grandeur of self-sacrifice on the part of a sybarite.[11]

[11]*Under Western Eyes*, pp. 305–306.

Under Western Eyes is not, like *The Secret Agent,* a small and symmetrical triumph of controlled form. It sets itself few technical boundaries, yet occasionally overflows even these to leave momentary impressions of clumsiness. Certain scenes in the second and third parts, carried on the "deluge of dialogue," are much too long. In this middle section of the novel, moreover, Conrad sometimes fails to conceal his embarrassment in the presence of acute problems of point of view. And the elderly teacher of languages and unprofessional narrator (who shows himself such an expert novelist through most of the first part) creates unnecessary obstacles by raising the question of authority. For this naturally leads us to examine and question his. Should he not rather have pretended to that truest authority which has nothing to do with Jamesian logic, and which he phrases very well in the second sentence below?

> Wonder may be expressed at a man in the position of a teacher of languages knowing all this with such definiteness. A novelist says this and that of his personages, and if only he knows how to say it earnestly enough he may not be questioned upon the inventions of his brain in which his own belief is made sufficiently manifest by a telling phrase, a poetic image, the accent of emotion. Art is great! But I have no art, and not having invented Madame de S——, I feel bound to explain how I came to know so much about her.[12]

The source and breadth of a narrator's information is of little importance as such. An example of looseness will serve, which would doubtless have caused James to groan. The nominal authority for the early St. Petersburg chapters is Razumov's diary, a diary which for the reader scarcely exists. This authority is obviously exceeded when the narrator enters Prince K——'s study, there to discover him "sitting sadly alone." The one thing of importance here violated, however, is the reader's intimate identification with Razumov. The instance is trivial and serves to remind us that Conrad too could forget about that diary. (Though it presumably was a protective, interposed instrument of no little use to his imagining.) A far more radical clumsiness—a clumsiness almost amusing in such a great novel—occurs in the first pages of Part III, as the narrator shuttles back and forth between Razumov's subjective view and his own eyewitness report. And there is to be sure the classic moment of awkwardness when (p. 317) the narrator walks into his own narrative by coming into Razumov's line of vision.

[12]*Ibid.,* p. 162.

But these are small flaws in the surface of a major success. The narrative method evidently worked, since it helped or at least permitted Conrad to dramatize his major scenes, rather than report them; and helped him to achieve his meaning without recourse to *The Secret Agent*'s heavy verbal irony. The method (in its combination of the meditative and the dramatic, the personal and the objective) is in part a development of that used in *Lord Jim*. It represents a serious effort to extend the possibilities of first-person narration without losing most of its generic advantages.* The teacher of languages is, unlike the Marlow of *Lord Jim*, the only narrator of the novel. But he manages to function at certain times as third-person omniscient observer, at other times as first-person eyewitness-participant. The first part, though based on a "document," is as forthright and as economical as the opening chapters of *Lord Jim*. It can evoke the assassination in a few paragraphs (here really relying, of course, on more than the document) and can present Razumov and his plight in a few pages.

The relative expertness of *Under Western Eyes* shows itself in the swiftness with which Conrad escapes nominal limitations, and converts a narrow point of view to, functionally, an ampler one. Thus the narrator who begins by disclaiming "the possession of those high gifts of imagination and expression" achieves, by page 12, all the dramatic power of the traditional observing point of view. Already he has made us forget that "documentary evidence" and even made us forget himself. So too Haldin's narrative-within-narrative report (through dialogue) of the assassination becomes, after only a few lines, a direct dramatizing of the event: intervening voices are silenced. In Part II Conrad again quickly disposes of his nominal authority (that Nathalie Haldin is telling the narrator about her visit to the Chateau Borel) and substitutes a dramatic third-person account of the event. We thus at least escape the weary game of quotation marks within quotation marks that mars *Lord Jim* and especially *Chance*. The particular technical compromise was one designed to satisfy both the reader (with his desire for dramatic immediacy) and the author (with his need for a literal detachment in space or time). Through certain scenes the reader appears to be experiencing life directly in a fictional present. But for the writer these protective screens still secretly existed: that the time is really past, that the imagination is at double or triple remove from the scene, that voices and documents are interposed.

---

*Among the generic advantages: eyewitness credibility and the authority of spoken voice, ease and naturalness of time-shift and transition, freedom to select only a few details or incidents. It can be a great relief to have one's "omniscience" formally limited, as it must be here.

The curious interruption and leap forward to the "later on" of Councillor Mikulin's trial is a clue, if we needed one, that this vivid and violent drama is (for Conrad's imagination) in the past. But it is the narrator's function as obtuse participant and observer to give, from page 100 on, a strong sense that we are in a fictional present time: watching new persons unexpectedly appear and unexpected events unroll, speculating on Razumov's status, and living through the very drama of ambiguity and discovery. The teacher of languages again protests, at the outset of the second part, his lack of professional skill. He "would not even invent a transition," he says—while accomplishing with ease the major transition from Councillor Mikulin's "Where to?" to the society of Nathalie Haldin and her mother.

At this point the narrative contracts to a very slow-moving present. We must wait some thirty-five pages for a further hint that Razumov and Nathalie Haldin may meet, sixty-seven pages for them to come face to face, seventy-two pages for those words that will send Razumov reeling against the wall. The delay is doubtless excessive. But some delay was certainly needed to make acceptable the melodramatic *donnée:* that Razumov will be sought out and admired by the sister of the man he betrayed. The illusion of presentness also permits the narrator's blundering unconscious ironies. For he is reconstructing a time when the first part of his narrative was unwritten. So in his fussy, innocent way he too can send Razumov reeling, as when he bluntly remarks: "There was something peculiar in the circumstances of his arrest. You no doubt know the whole truth. . . ." The last interview of Razumov and Nathalie Haldin is, as much as any scene in fiction, happening "now." And for the reader watching that scene the narrator's presence may seem unimportant; may even be forgotten. But his presence, and the fact that this interview nominally occurred in the past, were extremely important to Conrad. They permitted him to keep his saving distance, and so permitted him to write coherently of violence and without embarrassment of passion.

One of the great dangers of an obtuse narrator and Jamesian fool is, of course, the invitation to write imperceptive prose for the sake of accurate characterization. The danger would seem most severe where the general mode is realistic, as it is in *Under Western Eyes.* But this is a problem that James, Gide, Mann, Ford, and others have solved, and Conrad here solves it with little waste of time. A few brief passages suggest in their phrasing the narrator's old-maidish side. It comes out even in his comments on his lack of professional skill. "In the conduct of an invented story there are, no doubt, certain proprieties to be observed for the sake of clearness and effect." But from such a passage the narrator moves very quickly to an efficient, evocative prose not unlike that of James. "Mr. Razumov's record, like the open book of fate, revives for me the memory of that day as something startlingly pitiless in its freedom from all forebodings." Only a few pages after this he attains the major accent and lucid controlled irony of the Peter Ivanovitch portrait. Admittedly such a narrator was incapable of the strange rich connotative effects and subtly disturbing rhythms of *Lord Jim.* And perhaps Conrad too was incapable of them by now. But this self-effacing and more rational prose has the great merit of not interfering with the drama of ideas or with the drama of betrayal and redemption. The narrator's style was natural to Conrad, as the style of *The Secret Agent* was not. And it is probably capable of accomplishing a greater variety of effects. The prose style too points to the remarkable control Conrad kept, in *Under Western Eyes,* over very strong personal feelings. This exciting novel is also a triumph of intelligence.

Conrad himself remarked that the old teacher of languages was useful to him in several ways, and so must be useful to the reader: "in the way of comment and by the part he plays"; as an eyewitness to "produce the effect of actuality"; as a friend and listener for Miss Haldin, "who otherwise would have been too much alone and unsupported to be perfectly credible."[13] Conrad succeeds, we may repeat, in making the narrator's comment nearly always dramatic: a difficult and important achievement. His editorials on the Russian character and on Western rectitude may well reflect Conrad's cool views. But they are so timed and so phrased as to help create sympathy for the despised and the damned. And this too is, to recapitulate, a triumph of art and integrity. For the Russians also are human. "The obligation of absolute fairness was imposed on me historically and hereditarily, by the peculiar experience of race and family, in addition to my primary conviction that truth alone is the justification of any fiction which makes the least claim to the quality of art or may hope to take its place in the culture of men and women of its time."

This slightly graceless sentence from the Author's Note holds for me an accent of high sincerity.

---

[13]Author's Note.

R. W. B. Lewis

The Current of Conrad's Victory

The opening sentences of *Victory* introduce us half-playfully to a number of "close relations," the surprising similarities between seeming contrasts—coal and diamonds, the practical and the mystical, the diffused and the concentrated, an island and a mountain. All of them have their literal and thematic importance in the story, which describes a profound conflict rooted in opposition and likeness, and which has to do with coal, diamonds and an island; but the first effect of such dialectical teasing is the imparted sense of enlargement and creativity, of some idea or insight being made to grow. The last sentences of *Victory*, and especially its last word, are something else again:

> "And then, your Excellency [says good Captain Davidson], I went away. There was nothing to be done there."
> "Clearly," assented the Excellency.
> Davidson, thoughtful, seemed to weigh the matter in his mind, and then murmured with placid sadness:
> "Nothing!"

Between that initial sense of conceptual growth, with its cautious jocularity, and the thoughtful sadness of the closing negation there lies the truth of *Victory*, and its reality.

Victory is, in fact, a novel intimately concerned with questions of truth and reality, as it is with lies and illusion. Those big considerations force themselves on the imagination of the characters, and hence upon

Reprinted with the permission of Wayne State University Press, from Twelve Original Essays on Great English Novels *edited by Charles Shapiro, pp.* 203–31, © 1960 by Charles Shapiro.

that of the reader; for it is that kind of novel, the kind Conrad normally attempted to write. In his preface to *The Nigger of the Narcissus,* Conrad defined art as the effort to render the highest justice "to the visible universe, by bringing to light the truth, manifold and one, underlying its every aspect." That creative ambition found an exact analog in the experience narrated in *The Nigger of the Narcissus* itself, in the story's movement from the emphasized darkness of the ship's nighttime departure to the sunlit morning that greets its arrival in the English channel—after a voyage featured by the crew's effort to bring to light the truth and reality incarnate in the dying dark man, James Wait. And measured by Conrad's own standard, *Victory* achieves the conditions of art; for the manifold *and* unitary truth of things is just what Conrad succeeds in making real and visible, and what the persons of his island drama are most vitally concerned with. How the process is managed in this particular instance is the subject of present examination. But we have first to take a hard pull on our intellectual reins.

Revisiting *Victory* today, one cannot help being struck by its "existentialist" qualities—by how much it shares the intellectual preoccupations and postures notable in continental literature during recent decades. Here, for instance, is an elaborated image of human isolation: the isolation not only of man from man, but even more of man from his metaphysical environment—Axel Heyst, the rootless drifter, who has settled alone upon a singularly remote little island, near an abandoned coal mine, there to meditate in silence his late father's reflections upon "the universal nothingness" and "the unknown force of negation." Here, too, is the familiar counter-attack upon metaphysical isolation, the unsteady impulse towards human fellowship—those compassionate gestures towards Morrison and the girl called Lena which belie Heyst's habitual detachment and are the source of his misfortunes and maybe of his redemption. Here is the articulated obsession with the feeling of existence and of non-existence, as clues both to character and action. "If you were to stop thinking of me, I shouldn't be in the world at all," Lena says to Heyst; and, "I am he who is—" announces plain Mr. Jones, in a breath-taking moment which, in context, has an overpowering propriety. Here are modes of nihilism yielding to modes of self-annihilation, in the oddly similar catastrophes of both hero and villain. Here, in short, is a tale of violence that oscillates richly between the fundamental mysteries of being and nothing. Conrad, we are inclined to say, is the still insufficiently acknowledged grandfather of the most recent literary generation.

To say so is not necessarily to praise Conrad; and it is more likely, indeed, to impose upon him a false identity. *Victory* is not—and it cannot be discussed as—a novel of ideas, for example, in the manner of Malraux's *Les Noyers de L'Altenburg*. Nor is it a calculated work of metaphysical revolt, like Camus's *The Plague*. Conrad did of course display attitudes, and he had a stiff little set of convictions. But E. M. Forster has rightly, if unsympathetically, made the point that Conrad had no "creed"—no coherent order of intellectual principles; and no more than other novelists writing on English soil did Conrad possess that occasional French and German talent for making the war of thought itself exciting. He wanted to exploit the power of words, as he said, in order "to make you hear, to make you feel—before all to make you *see*"; and the end of each of his best novels was simply its own composition. He did not believe with Malraux that art is "a rectification of the universe, a way of escaping from the human condition"; and he would scarcely have understood Camus's parallel and derivative contention that "the novel is born simultaneously with the spirit of rebellion and expresses, on the aesthetic plane, the same ambition." *Victory* dramatizes basic aspects of truth and being; but as regards the human condition, its main aim is only to observe it in the way of art—with that idle but no less intense and sustained attention for which Conrad accurately thought he had a natural ability, and with which he recalled observing the living model for *Victory*'s heroine.

The novel's final word—"Nothing!"—is, accordingly, less a cry of appalled metaphysical recognition than the quiet acknowledgement that the adventure is over and the art that described it has peacefully exhausted itself. It is in the mood less of Camus's Caligula than of Shakespeare's Hamlet: "The rest is silence." The drama is done, and everybody who had a significant part in it is dead. Lena is dead, accidentally shot by Mr. Jones. Heyst has died by fire; Jones has died by water; and both deliberately, as it seems. Ricardo has been killed by Jones's second try at him; and Pedro has been dispatched by Wang, the houseboy. "There are more dead in this affair," Davidson remarks to the Excellency, "than have been killed in many of the battles of the last Achin war." The bungalow and the other two houses are burned to ashes; the boat has drifted out to sea; a corpse lies rotting on the scorched earth. To close the account, only the word "nothing" needs to be uttered.

And yet. If there is no metaphysical vision or purpose at work in the novel, there can nevertheless be felt running through it something like a metaphysical tide. Or better, perhaps, one senses the active presence, the dangerous undertow, of a metaphysical current giving the story its energy and its direction. In the same way, if the tale is not plainly intended as an allegory, one feels in it nevertheless something like an allegorical swelling, as though everything were about to become bigger than itself. That very impression affects the nerves of the persons in the book. "I have a peculiar feeling about this," says Mr. Jones. "It's a different thing. It's a sort of test." In the long list of Conrad's writings, *Victory* also comes to us as a different thing and a sort of test. It is Conrad's test of the nature of fiction: in general, of the ability of drama to move towards allegory while retaining intact its dramatic form and essence; and in particular, the ability of fiction to move towards drama while retaining its identity as fictional narrative. It is a test of the way truth and reality can become the subject-matter of a novel which hangs on to its novelistic nature. And the result, in my judgment, is indicated by the last word Conrad actually did write to this book, as he tells us: the single word of the title.

Victory (1915) is itself the last of those works both Conrad and his critics have agreed to call major; and it ranked with *Nostromo* (1904) as Conrad's personal favorite. Conrad's appraisal of his writings was, I think, both sound and suggestive. He always had a special fondness for *The Nigger of the Narcissus* (1897), recognizing it for what it was, his first genuine artistic accomplishment; and his satisfaction with *The Secret Agent* (1907) was grounded correctly in his belief that he had succeeded, in that novel, in treating "a melodramatic subject ironically," as he wrote in the copy he gave his friend Richard Curle. But he disagreed with readers and critics who thought that *Lord Jim* (1900) was his best book; he felt the tale did not justify the great length of the novel, and suspected that he should have stuck to his original idea, which was to restrict the narrative to the pilgrim ship episode. The most he could say for *Under Western Eyes* (1910) was "rather good." We should probably speak more warmly, but the pain of composition clings to the pages of *Under Western Eyes;* and the congealing of the action (for example, in Part III) is for long stretches greater than all the interpolated reflections on the art of fiction can overcome. About *Chance* (1913), in a manner not uncommon with authors, he began to talk deprecatingly the moment it became so huge a success. But he remained steadfast in his conviction that his two supreme efforts were the vast tale of the South American seaboard and the tight little story of Axel Heyst.

Surely he was right. *Nostromo* was, as Conrad knew, his largest canvas and his "most anxiously meditated work." It is also one of the greatest novels in English, with a greatness so complex and extensive that only belatedly and partially has it become appreciated. *Victory* is a triumph of a different kind, of a nearly opposite kind. Here Conrad has presented almost all the themes that interested him, but he has refracted those themes through the closely observed conduct of a tiny group of people in a tiny and absolutely isolated setting. *Nostromo* and *Victory* thus stand in a relation similar to the relation between *King Lear* and *Othello* (or perhaps like that between *The Possessed* and *Crime and Punishment*). Both *Nostromo* and *King Lear* comprehend more of the world and of human experience than the mind can comfortably contemplate; both are made up of a variety of parallel plots and involve several different groups of persons; in each we discover what Francis Fergusson calls "action by analogy," and the action so richly exposed in its multiplicity of modes reveals something not only about the individuals concerned but about the hidden drift of history, the secret and tragic movement of the universe. Both works engage the artist's most disturbing power—the prophetic power, which is of course not the ability to read the particular and immediate future, but the ability to read the future implicit in every grave and serious time, the future man is perennially prone to. In *Victory*, on the other hand, as in *Othello*, the action emerges directly from the peculiar temperaments of a few eccentric individuals. What happens, both artistically and psychologically, happens as a result of the impact of one unique personality upon another. This is not to deny any largeness to *Victory*; it is only to identify the source of the special largeness it does reveal. It is to say that the novel shows an allegorical swelling rather than an allegory, and that the creative force is less a pre-existent design the characters are re-enacting (for example, the myth of Eden, of the man and the woman in the garden and the invasion by the serpent) than the jarring effect of the human encounters.

The germ of *Nostromo* was an anecdote, the theft of a lighter-full of silver. But the germ of *Victory* seems to have been the remembered look of several unrelated persons glimpsed at sundry times and in sundry places. *Nostromo* houses characters enough for half a dozen novels; but it says something about Conrad's attitude towards them that he took most of their names from an old book of memoirs (G. F. Masterman's *Seven Eventful Years in Paraguay,* published in 1869) which gossiped about people called Carlos Gould, Monygham, Decoud, Fidanza, Barrios and Mitchell (*sic*). Conrad's inventive power in *Nostromo,* I am suggesting, was mainly or at least primarily directed to the exposure of action through plot. In *Victory,* however, we remark a thinness, almost a casualness, of plot invention; for Conrad's attention here was directed initially towards people—towards the exposure of action through character. The distinction is exaggerated, and with luck we can make it collapse; but for the moment it can be helpful. It is intended, in any

case, as a slight revision of the wonderfully fertile distinction offered by
Jacques Maritain, in *Creative Intuition in Art and Poetry*—the distinction between "the poetry of the novel" and "the poetry of the theater."
The latter, Maritain argues, is essentially the poetry of the action; action
comes first in the dramatic composition, and other elements—character,
especially—are subordinated to and controlled by the shape of the action, which it is their chief function to illuminate. The poetry of the
novel, Maritain continues, is the poetry of the agent, for the aim of
fiction is not so much to present an action as to shed light upon the
human heart. The incidents in a novel are accordingly selected in order
to illuminate the peculiar and representative nature of individual human
beings. M. Maritain's remarks and my respectful revision of them help
explain the sense in which *Victory* is a test of the nature of fiction. For
the "agents" of the book did come first in Conrad's planning and in his
writing. But by his manipulation of his characters, Conrad brought into
being an action virtually invulnerable in its design.

"Conrad was fond of discussing characters in *Victory*," Curle
reports; and in his author's note, Conrad discusses little else. He shares
with us the memories that went into the making of the novel: a professional card-sharper he had seen once in the West Indies in 1875; the
silent wide-eyed girl in a café orchestra in the South of France; the
wandering Swedish gentleman who became "the physical and moral
foundation of my Heyst." "It seems to me but natural," Conrad says,
"that those three buried in the corner of my memory should suddenly
get out into the light of the world." The reference was actually to the
three bad men, Mr. Jones and Martin Ricardo and Pedro; but it applies
equally to the three key figures in the story. They gathered together
irresistibly in Conrad's imagination, just as they gather together for the
culminating experience of each of their lives on Heyst's island. They
are made known to us exactly through the process of gathering. And
indeed the first and most obvious way to chart the unfolding scheme of
the book is to point to the important moments in that process.

We meet Axel Heyst on the first page. We hear of Lena thirty-six
pages later in Mrs. Schomberg's reluctant mutter to Davidson: "There
was even one English girl." Mr. Jones makes his appearance fifty-five
pages later yet: "a guest who arrived one fine morning by mail-boat
. . . a wanderer, clearly, even as Heyst was." Conrad then devotes
nearly seventy pages to acquainting us with the three desperadoes, and
with the critical differences between them. But even before he begins
that section, the gathering process has been at work in the meeting and
the drawing together of Heyst and Lena, and their flight to the island
refuge. The entire group of major characters (the Schombergs, of

course, excluded) is not assembled in a single place until a little more than half-way through the book: when Wang interrupts the moment of deepest intimacy between Heyst and Lena to announce that a boat (containing, as we learn, Mr. Jones and his henchmen) is approaching the jetty. From that instant, the whole of the novel is caught up in the collision of personalities—in what Henry James (speaking about one of Ibsen's plays) called the lunging of ego against ego, the passionate rocking of soul against soul; every ego against every ego, in Conrad's masterful treatment of it, and every soul against every soul. From the instant the boat is sighted—or more accurately, from the instant Heyst goes down to the jetty to stare in amazement at the spectacle of the three white men drifting in from nowhere, seemingly more dead than alive—Conrad's complex artistic purpose becomes clear and begins to fulfill itself. The individual characters, explored individually or in small combinations, now meet and join in an adventure which becomes an action larger and more significant than any of them. The novel, that is, begins to assume the defining quality of drama.

Throughout the course of it, however, Conrad continues to exploit the peculiar resources of the novel, for the traditional aims of the novelist; but he does so, at the same time, as a way of heightening and solidifying the dramatic design. In elaborating the distinction I have mentioned, Jacques Maritain observes that since the shape of the action is determining in a drama, contingencies and coincidences and simple accidents have no place there; but that these devices are proper to fiction, since they can be exactly the occasion for some special insight into character. During the latter half of *Victory,* the plot is heavily dependent upon a series of "evitable" incidents, of which two may be cited as typical: the theft of Heyst's gun by Wang, and the shooting of Lena by Mr. Jones. The latter is pure accident: Jones had intended to kill Martin Ricardo. The former is a contingency—Wang might have had a gun of his own, or Heyst another revolver hidden away somewhere. Each incident is important to the plot as plotted. But alternatives can easily be imagined, and neither incident seems indispensable to the larger purpose. Yet both incidents serve to shed light on the characters involved and are insofar novelistically justified; and in the light they shed, a truth and a reality begin to appear, as elements towards which an action is steadily in motion.

These incidents, in short, are literally accidental, but they are symbolically inevitable and dramatically appropriate. The theft of the gun tells us a good deal about the curiously hidden nature of the house-boy, his swift and agile selfishness with its portion of quiet cruelty; and it reinforces the sense pervading the world of the book, that in it the distance between men is nearly absolute. At the same time, by rendering Heyst physically defenseless, it provides an "objective correlative" for his more fundamental defenselessness, that of a man of thought like himself in the hour of necessary action. The time spent in puzzling and worrying over the absence of the gun is time artistically well spent. The death of Lena has a still higher degree of propriety. Mr. Jones's bullet, though aimed at Ricardo, only grazed Ricardo's temple before burying itself in Lena's heart, just "under the swelling breast of dazzling and sacred whiteness"—the accident is compounded by the terrible chance that the bullet should strike her exactly there. Yet we need little instruction from the Freudians to perceive that the accident probably masked an act of deepest deliberation. Towards Ricardo, Mr. Jones felt only fury mixed with a lively sense of danger; but towards Lena, towards any woman, he felt the much more destructive emotion of radical disgust. The shooting of Lena is one of the last and most meaningful of the gestures by which we take the full measure of plain Mr. Jones—the evil ascetic, the satanic figure whose satanism springs from a loathing of women and a horror of sex. (Graham Greene, who has written a short essay called "Plain Mr. Jones," and who is indebted to Conrad on many counts, has provided a comparable image in Pinkie Brown, the inflamed ascetic of *Brighton Rock*.) And in the mode of her death, we have the final revelation and indeed the vindication of Lena's character. Hers is the touching figure of the young woman of smudged virtue who prays she may lose everything for the sake of the man she loves (again, a figure we encounter in Graham Greene). She has drawn upon herself the death that threatened Axel Heyst. To do so is not only a part of her character. It is a part of her plan.

Each of the main figures in *Victory* has his or her private plan; and in this respect, *Victory* too, like *Nostromo*, has a number of plots—as many as the number of central characters; the plot in each case being what happens at last to the individual plan. As each plan is lit up for us, so much more of the action comes into view. In human terms, the separate plans are catastrophically irreconcilable, and in their difference they provide the "manifold" truth—to use Conrad's word—that the novel brings to light. But artistically, they form a living pattern of parallels and contrasts, and so provide the unitary truth Conrad equally envisaged.

Each of these secret programs of conduct is rooted in the mystery of one or two absolute characteristics. Schomberg's malice, for example, is an absolute trait of character, as unmotivated as the malice of Iago. Like Iago's hatred of Othello, Schomberg's hatred of Axel Heyst can pretend to a specific reason: Heyst's snatching away of the girl, which led to the funny Faulknerian madhouse involving Schomberg and the orchestra leader Zangiacomo, over which Conrad used to laugh reminiscently. But the hatred existed already, existed even before the episode, which Schomberg so evilly misrepresented, of Heyst and poor Morrison. Schomberg's private plot, rooted in his malice, is the business of his so-called revenge upon Heyst, along with the business of diverting the outlaws from his own hotel to the safe distance of Heyst's island. In its vicious way, it is successful, but not because it has anything to do with the facts about Heyst and Lena. Schomberg's plot is strictly his own creation; it is not nourished to any real extent by external circumstances. The same is true of his malignancy. It is a key factor in releasing the terrible events of the book; but it is not developed by outside pressures, it is *revealed* by them. Thus it is with the determining features of the other people in *Victory*. For here, as is customary in Conrad's work, the characters do not grow, they only grow more visible. That is the precise effect of their mutual impact.

Mr. Jones is perhaps the most fascinating instance in the novel of the motion towards visibility, if only because it is the most paradoxical. What becomes fully and finally visible about him is a kind of absence, a nothingness. His plan is the least reconcilable of all the plans, and hence the most irreducible symptom of the "manifold" aspect of *Victory*: because Mr. Jones's plan opposes not only the substance of all the others but the very terms of their existence. Ricardo, we remember, has his own particular reasons—reasons he cannot disclose to Mr. Jones —for urging the invasion of Heyst's island; and no doubt some dumb dream of conquest occupies the primitive skull of Pedro. But the mission of Mr. Jones undercuts all that. It has to do with the condition of his being, which is as it were a mockery of being itself. Heyst reports to Lena on his conversation with Jones:

> "I suppose you would like to know who I am?" he asked me.
>   I told him I would leave it to him, in a tone which, between gentlemen, could have left no doubt in his mind. He raised himself on his elbow—he was lying down on the campbed—and said:
>   "I am he who is—."

"No use asking me what he meant, Lena," Heyst adds. "I don't know." What Jones meant was probably a theatrical blasphemy. In very similar words, according to the Old Testament, God announced his name and his nature to his chosen people: "I am," or "I am that I am." Jones, of course, is not god-like, and especially not god-like in the sense of representing the source of being itself. He is devil-like—his character bulges in the direction of the devil (he is not *the* devil, any more than *Victory* is an allegory); and exactly because he represents the source of non-being.

The association with Satan gratifies Mr. Jones immensely. He describes, in an echo from the Book of Job, his habit of "coming and going up and down the earth"; and Heyst replies that he has "heard that sort of story about someone else before." Jones at once gives Heyst a ghastly grin, claiming that "I have neither more nor less determination" than "the gentleman you are thinking of." But the nature and end of his determination emerge from a later allusion to the devil. Jones speculates for Heyst's benefit that a man living alone, as Heyst had been living, would "take care to conceal [his] property so well that the devil himself—." Heyst interrupts with a murmured "Certainly."

> Again, with his left hand, Mr. Jones mopped his frontal bone, his stalk-like neck, his razor jaws, his fleshless chin. Again, his voice faltered and his aspect became still more gruesomely malevolent, as of a wicked and pitiless corpse.

Those last four words summarize the character of Mr. Jones and point to his unswerving purpose: he is not only deathly, he is the cause that death is in others. To Schomberg, too, Jones had seemed "to imply some sort of menace from beyond the grave"; and in Heyst's first view of him, Jones is "sitting up [in the boat], silent, rigid and very much like a corpse." At the outset of their duel, Jones seems to exert a greater force of sheer existence than Heyst; for Heyst, as he confesses mournfully in language highly reminiscent of one of Hawthorne's isolated men, has lived too long among shadows. But Heyst's determining quality has only been lying dormant; he is like the indolent volcano, to which he is lightly compared on the second page of the book; he is moving—though moving too late and too slowly—towards existence and reality. Jones's characteristic movement is all in the other direction.

The force in Jones is all negative, though not the less emphatic for being so. That is why he hates and fears women, for they are fertility incarnate and the literal source of life. Jones's particular and personal plot is not really to seize Heyst's alleged treasures, but to inflict his deathiness upon others. He comes as an envoy of death, disguised as an envoy of the living: of death not in the sense of murder, but in the sense of a fundamental hostility to existence. He is the champion of the anti-real, and he arrives at just the moment when Heyst, because of the presence and love of Lena, is feeling "a greater sense of reality than he had ever known in his life." Jones's plan, too, is superficially successful: everyone he has brushed against on the island is dead. Jones is dead also; but he has not been killed, he has simply shrunk, collapsed, disintegrated. He has reached the limit of his true condition. And what is visible of him at the end is exactly the outward signs of that condition. "The water's very clear there," Davidson tells the Excellency; "and I could see him huddled up on the bottom between two piles, like a heap of bones in a blue silk bag, with only the head and feet sticking out."

Mr. Jones's most astute enemy in the book is not Heyst but the girl Lena, though Jones and Lena never in fact confront one another. But Lena is the one person able to understand not only the threat represented by the invaders, but the very threat of the threat; and she understands it so well that, as things develop, she can formulate her own plot and purpose to herself with exactness—to "capture death—savage, sudden, irresponsible death, prowling round the man who possessed her." Lena stands for a possibility of life. Yet curiously enough, her role as the actual source of Heyst's sense of being is rendered less visible —rendered, that is, with less apparent success—than are the deadly negations of Mr. Jones. Lena is the one member of the cast who remains in partial darkness. Many critics have remarked upon this, and some have gone on to say that Conrad rarely had much luck with his women. But his achievement elsewhere is not always unimpressive: Winnie Verloc, in *The Secret Agent,* seems to me one of the most compelling females in modern literature; and one has little difficulty making out the attractive features of Emily Gould and Flora de Barral, in *Nostromo* and *Chance* respectively. It may even be that a kind of haziness, a fragility of substance was intended in the portrayal of Lena. She *is* like that, and the frailty of her being determines the nature of her plot. For her aim is precisely to win for herself a greater measure of reality, by forcing upon the man she loves a greater recognition of her. She lives in his acknowl-edgment of her: "If you were to stop thinking about me I shouldn't be in the world at all. . . . I can only be what you think I am." This is a trifle unfortunate, since Heyst, the only human being who could have seen Lena, can never manage to see quite enough. Richard Curle observes nicely about Lena that she is "the supreme example of a 'one-man' woman, so supreme that even the reader is kept out of the secret." Heyst peers at her in the half-light, and we peer over his shoulder, dimly discerning a creature of considerable but only guessed-at bodily appeal and intense but only partially communicated spiritual desire.

Her desire is stated plainly enough for us, as it takes form after Ricardo's attempt to rape her. From that moment onward, "all her energy was concentrated on the struggle she wanted to take upon her-self, in a great exaltation of love and self-sacrifice." And we know enough about her history to find that exaltation plausible. We have heard of her mother's desertion of her father, of her father's career as a small-time musician and of his removal to a home for incurables; we have heard of her bleak childhood and adolescence, her blurred unhappy life with a travelling orchestra; we can easily imagine what Heyst's compassion must have meant to her. "I am not what they call a good girl," she has said; and through Heyst's impression of her, we are struck by her mixture of misery and audacity. She alone fully understands that it is Schomberg who has put the outlaws on Heyst's trail, and she can comprehend the hotel-keeper's motiveless motive. Lena's plot, accordingly, is the most coherent of all the plots, and the most important. It is also the most private, since it requires of her that she lie both to the man she hates and the man she loves. She is altogether successful, at least as successful as Schomberg or Mr. Jones. She does disarm Ricardo, literally and psychologically; the dagger she takes from him is indeed "the spoil of vanquished death" and "the symbol of her victory." By dividing Ricardo from Jones, she creates a situation in which, as the demonically brilliant Jones instantly realizes, Ricardo must be killed; and through a chain-reaction, she is responsible also for the death of Pedro and Jones himself. All this we know, understand and can rehearse. But Conrad has nonetheless not finally managed to fulfill his ambition with respect to Lena. He has not made us see Lena completely. Between her and ourselves, there falls a shadow. It is, of course, the shadow of Axel Heyst.

If the victory is Lena's—if her end, as Conrad insisted, is triumphant—the major defeat recorded in the novel is that of Heyst. His is the ultimate failure, and for the reason he gives in almost the last words we hear him speak: "Ah, Davidson, woe to the man whose heart has not learned while young to hope, to love—and to put its trust in life." But that very statement demonstrates that Heyst, by acknowledging his failure and perceiving its cause, has in the literary manner of speaking been saved. He is, at the last, completely in touch with truth. And similarly, if Heyst's personal plan—which is not only to rid the island of its invaders and to protect Lena, but also to join with Lena in an experience of full reality—if that plan is the least successful plan in the book, Heyst is nonetheless the true and steady center of the novel from its beginning to its end. So central is Heyst within the rich composition of *Victory*, that neither his character nor his conduct may be clearly seen apart from that composition. They are identified only through a series of analogies and contrasts, and as the vital center of the book's design.

As analysis moves to the figure of Axel Heyst, it moves of necessity from the Many to the One—from the many separated individuals with their irreconcilable differences of purpose to the pattern in which they seem to echo and reflect and repeat one another. It is the felt flow of the Many into the One that accounts for the feeling one has of a strong metaphysical current running deep through the novel, of very real human beings and events gathering together in a way that suggests an allegory of universal proportions. Let it be emphasized again that we have to do with a process, not with an imposition. And as it develops, we begin to detect parallels between contrasting and inimical elements, continuities between divisions—and by the power of the book's current, more radical contrasts between newly observed parallels. At the center is Axel Heyst, whose entire being—*artistically,* within the actual pages of the book—is created by the play of likeness and difference.

We must, accordingly, approach Heyst by way of those relationships—which is to reconsider some of the persons already inspected, but to consider them now not in their enormous differences, but in their unexpected similarities: an undertaking the first page of *Victory* (with its references to the similarities between coal and diamonds, an island and a mountain) has warned us would be the key to the novel's meaning. Between Lena and Ricardo, for example, between the mystically devoted young woman and the thick-headed roughneck who plunges headlong through the blue serge curtain to assault her, an unexpected likeness is uncovered. It is a fatality in Ricardo's crude imagination that he should exaggerate it. "You and I are made to understand each other," he mumbles, after a stupor of surprise and admiration at the vigor of Lena's resistance. "Born alike, bred alike, I guess. You are not tame, Same here! You have been chucked out into this rotten world of 'ypocrits. Same here!" Because of his conviction of their likeness, Ricardo trusts Lena more simply and unquestioningly than Heyst trusts her; Ricardo trusts what there is in Lena of his own animal and prehensile nature, and he dies of that trust, as Heyst dies of mistrust. But within disastrous limits. Ricardo is right—he and Lena do have a good deal in common. "Perhaps because of the similarity of their miserable origin in the dregs of mankind," Lena realizes, "she had understood Ricardo perfectly." Even her physical strength and tenacity match his: "You have fingers like steel! Jiminy! You have muscles like a giant." That is scarcely the pathetic child seen through Heyst's impression of her, the child suffering helplessly the venomous pinchings of Mrs. Zangiacomo; and the ferocity of her response to Ricardo's attempted rape correctly suggests a ready perception, based on experience, of that kind of jungle behavior. It also suggests the strength in Lena which has been brought to the surface since the Zangiacomo days: brought to the surface and focused as a powerful instrument, through the effect upon her of Heyst.

An important ingredient in her strength is a talent for lying, exercised for the sake of truth. Ricardo is quite justified in attributing to Lena a duplicity equal to his own; he knows that both of them have had to become skilled in duplicity as the one indispensable resource in the world's hypocritical "game of grab." "Give the chuck to all this blamed 'ypocrisy," urges Ricardo. Lena seems to agree, and she embarks deceptively upon a plot to deceive Heyst—"her gentleman," as Ricardo calls him—which notably parallels Ricardo's systematic deception of *his* gentleman, Mr. Jones. It seems to Ricardo natural that Lena should lie to the man who has befriended her; such is the norm of behavior in the world he inhabits: that is, the world of *Victory*. It is what people do to each other in that world: witness Mrs. Schomberg's trickery of her own gentleman, her fat braggart of a husband. The cluster of duplicities has, up to a point, a common element, for each aims initially at the salvation of the man deceived. Mrs. Schomberg, when she helps frustrate her husband's plans (his "insane and odious passion") by helping Lena to escape, imagines she is keeping Schomberg out of serious trouble and preserving their wretched marriage. Ricardo's organization of the invasion of Heyst's island is a contrivance to rescue his chief from the habitual state of sloth into which Jones had fallen. To do so, Ricardo must cunningly keep silent about the presence on the island of a young woman; since, were Jones to hear about it, he would instantly abandon the adventure. Only later does Ricardo's helpful deceit deepen into betrayal. And as to Lena, "she was not ashamed of her duplicity," because "nothing stood between the enchanted dream of her existence and a cruel catastrophe but her duplicity." She will deceive every one, and she will especially deceive Heyst; she will wear the mask of infidelity to save the life of the man towards whom her fidelity is the very assurance of her existence.

The relationship between Lena and Ricardo thus illuminates one of the major themes of the novel—the theme of truth-telling, and the significance of truth-telling, as a value, in the scheme of human behavior. By the same token, Lena and Ricardo illuminate the character of Axel Heyst; for it is almost a weakness in Heyst that—at the opposite extreme from Mr. Jones and his self-association with the Father of Lies—he has an absolute regard for truth. He is so obsessed with truth that he becomes literally disempowered when confronted with lies; and he is so inflexible towards truth that only lies can save him. Even more than the theft of his gun, as it seems, it is the lies Schomberg has spread about Heyst's treatment of Morrison that, when they belatedly reach Heyst's ears, succeed finally in rendering him defenseless by provoking in him the emotion of paralyzing disgust. His only defense thereafter is the multiple duplicity of Lena.

It is not inappropriate that such should be the case, for between Morrison and Lena, too, there is a revealing similarity. Lena shares with Ricardo a certain seamy background and a certain practical toughness; but with Morrison, the unfortunate master of the trading brig *Capricorn,* she has shared the magnanimity of Axel Heyst. The story of Morrison is a sort of rehearsal for the story of Lena; for like Lena, Morrison is not only the object; he is in a sense the victim of Heyst's compassion. Morrison is miraculously rescued by Heyst in a way that, as events work out, both leads to and makes plausible the rescue, not long after, of Lena; and the consequence in both cases is a fresh involvement, a chance for life, that results in fact in their death. Both look upon Heyst as a kind of god, especially because to both Heyst's conduct appears purely gratuitous, like the undeserved and disinterested mercy of God. It is not merely pity; Heyst's father had advised him to "cultivate that form of contempt which is called pity," but the salvaging of Morrison and the benevolent theft of Lena are due to no such calculated attitude. They reflect rather a temperament which, as we are told, was incapable of scorning any decent emotion—a temperament so fine and rare as to seem literally godlike to the bedeviled of the book's world. When Heyst offers Morrison the money to save the latter's boat, Morrison gazes at him as though "he expected Heyst's usual white suit of the tropics to change into a shining garment down to his toes . . . and didn't want to miss a single detail of the transformation." In the procedure typical of *Victory,* a reaction which will later become serious, complex and tragic is presented in the early pages in simple and partly comic tonalities. Lena's reaction to Heyst's rescue of her is less extravagant and open-mouthed; but it partakes of a still deeper awe and of a genuinely self-sacrificial reverence.

In the same way, it is Morrison who first strikes the note, in his droll and touching way, which will develop into a theme close to the tragic heart of the book. Morrison wonders in panic if Heyst is joking about the money. Heyst asks austerely what he means, and Morrison is abashed.

> "Forgive me, Heyst. You must have been sent by God in answer to my prayer. But I have been nearly off my chump for three days with worry; and it suddenly struck me: 'What if it's the Devil who has sent him?' "
> "I have no connection with the supernatural," said Heyst graciously, moving on. "Nobody sent me. I just happened along."
> "I know better," contradicted Morrison.

That moment has its louder and more serious echo a couple of hundred pages later, when Heyst catches sight of Jones and his henchmen approaching the jetty. He stares at them in disbelief: "[He] had never been so much astonished in his life."

> The civilisation of the tropics could have nothing to do with it. It was more like those myths, current in Polynesia, of amazing strangers, who arrive at an island, gods or demons, bringing good or evil to the innocence of the inhabitants—gifts of unknown things, words never heard before.

"Gods or demons, bringing good or evil. . . ." Those ambiguous phrases greet the first glimpse Heyst and Jones have of each other; and they frame and give shape to the most telling of the patterns of similarity and contrast that *Victory* has to offer—the one that says most about Heyst himself, and the one that best reveals the drama of which he is the protagonist. Between Heyst and Jones, the differences are of radical dimensions. Heyst is a bringer of good (though the recipients of his gifts suffer evil by consequence). Jones is a bringer of evil (through his gift is the occasion of greatest good for Lena, and her victory). Heyst has some godlike element in his nature; but the insinuation makes him highly uncomfortable. Jones has a kind of private understanding with the Devil, and that insinuation never fails to excite him. But between Axel Heyst and plain Mr. Jones, there is a vibrant flow of analogies, a movement back and forth like electrical currents.

A likeness is registered at the instant Jones first turns up in the novel; a guest at Schomberg's hotel arriving from Celebes, "but generally, Schomberg understood, from up China Sea way; a wanderer clearly, even as Heyst was." Both men are drifters by profession—"I'll drift," Heyst had decided as a young man; both have occupied themselves for many years by "coming and going up and down the earth." Both men are gentlemen, in the conventional meaning of the word and within the book's definition as pronounced by Martin Ricardo: "That's another thing you can tell a gentlemen by, his freakishness. A gentleman ain't accountable to nobody, any more than a tramp on the roads." Heyst invokes a comparable notion: "I, Axel Heyst, the most detached of creatures in this earthly captivity, the veriest tramp on this earth. . . ." As gentlemen and as tramps, both Jones and Heyst are products of highly civilized society who have chosen the career of the rootless outsider. Both are well-born, perhaps aristocratic; they are elegant, sophisticated, mannerly; both have an excessive vein of fastidiousness, a too easily outraged austerity. And both are outcasts who in different ways are outside the law: Heyst by being in some manner beyond and above it, Jones by being several degrees beneath it. With one of his ghastly grins, during their first interview, Mr. Jones confesses to Heyst that the latter was not the man he had expected to meet. For he sees or thinks he sees, startlingly, *son semblable, son frè*re.

Jones misjudges Heyst just as Ricardo misjudges Lena, and with the same limited warrant. "We pursue the same ends," Jones remarks; and he argues that his presence on the island is neither more nor less "morally reprehensible" than Heyst's. Jones assumes that, like himself, Heyst is simply a gentlemanly scoundrel, sharing with him the impulse common to gifted men—the criminal impulse. About this mistake there is something as ridiculous as it is fatal; but Jones has intuited a fragment of the truth. Heyst does share with Jones a basic indifference to the habitual practices of society and to its moral verdicts. He appraises the world in terms nearly identical to those of Jones: "The world's a mad dog," Heyst tells Davidson. "It will bite you if you give it a chance." These two lean and handsome gentlemen, these radical drifters, have an extraordinary amount in common, and Jones's contention is justified—"Ah, Mr. Heyst . . . you and I have much more in common than you think." Jones and Heyst reflect each other with a sort of perfection, the way an object is reflected in a mirror. Each is the other seen wrong way round.

That is why they are dramatically indispensable one to the other —the visibility of each is dependent upon the presence of the other. They come from opposite ends of the universe, and they meet where opposites are made to meet: in a work of art. The strength of each often appears as an extension of the other's weakness and vice-versa; which is one reason why the conflict between them, as it assumes its form, seems to extend endlessly, to enlarge almost beyond the reach of human reckoning. It brushes the edge of allegory, and touches briefly on the outskirts of myth—one of "those myths, current in Polynesia, of amazing strangers . . . gods or demons." But the drama hangs on to its human vitality and its immediacy and continues to draw its force from the peculiar nature of the two men involved—the man of intellectual sensibility with an inadequate but incipient trust in life; and the man of occasional action with a strenuous but insufficiently examined faith in the power of death. Mr. Jones's tendency to sloth, which leaves him spread motionless over three chairs for hours at a time, is reflected in Heyst's long period of meditation on the hostility of thought to action, while he lounges on the verandah and smokes his cheroot. But Jones's condition has the terrible and explosive power of an ancient sin; and Heyst's skepticism is marred by a vein of tenderness. If Heyst had mistrusted life more completely, he would perhaps have been a better

match for Jones from the outset. As it is, the novel catches him at the
moment when mistrust is giving way to an urge toward reality and
communion.

He had long since, so he tells Jones during their last conversation,
divorced himself from the love of life; but then he adds, with painful
accuracy, "not sufficiently perhaps." So he acts and reacts without
"distinctness." His conception of the world, taken from his father, had
for too many years been of something "not worth touching, and perhaps
not substantial enough to grasp." The experience of Lena was beginning to put substance into the world; but Heyst can neither participate
fully in that experience nor resist it, for he has absorbed either too much
or too little of his father's doctrine that "the consolation of love" is the
cruelest of all the stratagems of life. He can still insist that "he who
forms a tie is lost," but his actual feeling is that he is about to find
himself, that Lena is giving him "a greater sense of his own reality than
he had ever known in his life."

Greater: but still inadequate to fit him for the challenge that arises.
For that challenge is exactly the embodiment of the challenge his father
had honorably faced. "With what strange serenity, mingled with terrors," Heyst thinks about his father, "had that man considered the
universal nothingness! He had plunged into it headlong, perhaps to
render death, the answer that faced one at every inquiry, more support-
able." It is only four pages later that Wang arrives to announce the
approach of a strange boat. And Mr. Jones, the corpse-like figure at the
tiller of the boat, is himself the harbinger and representative of that
"universal nothingness." He is the body of that death "that faced one
at every inquiry." Trapped between a warning skepticism and an un-
dernourished sense of reality, Heyst cannot emulate his father; cannot
make the plunge or launch the assault. All he can do, at the end, is to
take death upon himself, purgatorially, by fire.

But, if Heyst is unable to plunge, Jones (like Ricardo on his lower
level) plunges too incautiously. The sinister mission he engages on is
unsupported by the necessary amount of cold intelligence—of just that
kind of intelligence that Heyst possesses supremely. Heyst begins finally to exercise it at Jones's expense during their climactic interview,
after Heyst has learned the reason for the invasion of the
island—Schomberg's preposterous falsehood about treasures hidden on
it. At this instant, a reversal is effected, and Heyst takes command of
their relationship; it is his strength now which becomes visible because
of the revelation of Jones's weakness. "You seem a morbid, senseless
sort of bandit," Heyst says with weary contempt. "There were never in
the world two more deluded bandits—never! . . . Fooled by a silly

rascally innkeeper,'' he goes on remorselessly. ''Talked over like a pair of children with a promise of sweets.'' It is the logical weakness of Jones's asserted belief in universal fraudulence that it must contain in itself an element of the fraudulent. If he had been wholly convinced of the depravity of all the inhabitants of a wholly vicious world, Jones would have trusted less in the strength of his authority—his graveyard power—over Martin Ricardo; and he would not have overlooked the possibility of mere vulgar vindictiveness in Schomberg. He leapt too swiftly from sloth into action, in a way that, in retrospect, invests one of Heyst's casual pronouncements, made early in the book, with prophetic implications: ''Action is the devil.''

Heyst and Jones need each other for artistic visibility; but both of them need Lena, as she needs them, to make clear the full shape of the drama they have begotten between them, when the current of the novel carries them (this is one's impression) into a dimension beyond the dimension occupied by all the other persons in the book. The action disclosed by the effect of those three upon each other is the gradual location of that dimension, of the very domain of reality and truth. The domain lies somewhere between the dialectical stirrings of the book's first page and the observation of nothingness on its last—somewhere, as it turns out, between the intellectualism of Heyst and the deathiness of Jones. Between the two kinds of failure, Lena's victory is squeezed out in a way that is a victory both for her and for the novel in which she has her being. As against Jones, Lena has dedicated herself to the actual cause of living; and as against Heyst, she has seized with fingers of steel upon the immediate and necessary facts of behavior. Her practicality (again the book's first page is recalled) derives from a mystical exalta- tion that transcends the particular situation and attains to universal value while remaining sharply and intently focussed upon the single figure of Axel Heyst. Lena's accomplishment reflects the accomplishment of the novel. *Victory* is, in a sense, a reproach to the fascination with death of so much modern fiction. But even more, perhaps, it is an admonition about the tendency of both fiction and criticism to intellectualize the art—to lose the drama in the allegory; or to deform the art—to lose the novel in the drama. The form of *Victory* grows dramatic, and it gives forth intimations of allegory. But it remains faithful to its own nature, for it never makes the mistake of Mr. Jones—it never fails to take account of the variable and highly unpredictable character of individual human beings.

Eloise Knapp Hay

"The Artist of the Whole Matter"

The extent of Conrad's importance as a political novelist was first noticed in 1949, when George Orwell called him "one of the few true novelists that England possesses," representing "a sort of grown-upness and political understanding which would have been almost impossible to a native English writer at the time." Orwell classed Conrad with T. S. Eliot, Henry James, Joyce, and Yeats as foreigners "who in the present century civilized English literature and brought it back into contact with Europe, from which it had been almost severed for a hundred years."[1] G. D. H. Cole, who gave his opinion in the same collection of critiques on Conrad in which Orwell's appeared, singled out *The Secret Agent* and *Under Western Eyes* as having passed almost unnoticed among Conrad's works, although deserving of the highest regard.

If Orwell was right in suggesting that Conrad's political understanding enlarged and "civilized" the English point of view, it was

[1] In "Conrad's Place and Rank in English Letters," *Wiadomości* (London), April 10, 1949. Actually, Orwell's words seem almost a paraphrase of Ford Madox Ford's remark before Conrad's death: "Nevertheless, the works of Mr. Conrad that the present writer most tremendously remembers are *Heart of Darkness, Nostromo, Under Western Eyes*—that finest novel in the English language—and *The Secret Agent,* that immense failure of comprehension! Each of these is a political parable, and so, you might add, is *An Outpost of Progress;* and so, for the matter of that, is, with its atmosphere of Arab and Malay intrigue beneath the shadow of Dutch suzerainty, Mr. Conrad's first book, *Almayer's Folly"* (*Thus to Revisit*. [New York: Dutton, 1921], pp. 90–91). A few pages further on (p. 101), Ford adds: "Mr. Conrad, coming from Poland—even as Henry James coming from New England—has once more put Anglo-Saxondom into contact with the main stream of human art."

From The Political Novels of Joseph Conrad *by Eloise Knapp Hay, The University of Chicago Press.* © *1963 by Eloise Knapp Hay. Reprinted by permission.*

possible only because as a Pole Conrad symbolized a cause with which most Englishmen had instinctive sympathy, while at the same time he represented a people whose political outlook was in many ways utterly alien. The Poland known to the English throughout the greater part of the nineteenth century, according to E. H. Carr,

> represented both the essence of nationalism and the essence of democracy. The oppressors of Poland were the three traditional opponents, since the Congress of Vienna, of democracy and nationalism: Austria, Russia, and Prussia. France and Great Britain, who ruled over no subject races in Europe, were free to indulge the liberal sentiments which they professed by sympathizing with the subject Poles. . . . In the hands of the nineteenth century democrats the cause of Poland became a symbol of international righteousness.[2]

Conversely, the England admired by Polish patriots in the nineteenth century was a land that symbolized political hope, even for men who professed hopeless indifference. In the year before Conrad was naturalized as a British citizen (1886), he wrote from Singapore to his Polish friend Spiridion Kliszczewski, living in Cardiff, that the newspapers announcing the defeat of England's Liberal government (with its policy of friendship toward Russia) had given him reason for "expecting great things":

> I saw with pleasure the evidence of improved relations with Germany, the only power with whom an anti-Russian alliance would be useful, and even possible, for Great Britain. . . . Events are casting shadows, more or less distorted, shadows deep enough to suggest the lurid light of battlefields somewhere in the near future, but all those portents of great and decisive doings leave me in a state of despairing indifference: for whatever may be the changes in the fortunes of living nations, for the dead there is no hope. . . .[3]

The deceased nation had yet her scattered heirs, with their allegiance to mankind, if nothing else. In the same letter Conrad added,

> I agree with you that in a free and hospitable land even the most persecuted of our race may find relative peace and a certain amount of happiness, materially at least; consequently, I understood and readily accepted your reference to "Home." When speaking, writing or thinking in English, the word home always means for me the hospitable shores of Great Britain.

[2]*Michael Bakunin* (London: Macmillan, 1937), p. 139.
[3]Letter to Kliszczewski, Oct. 13, 1885, in G. Jean-Aubry, *Joseph Conrad: Life and Letters,* I (New York: Doubleday, Page, 1927) 80–81.

There was a side to Polish politics, however, which the English mind (the American mind as well), priding itself on liberalism and evolutionary progress, chose not to recognize and shrank away from whenever agitation for Polish freedom became too strong in Parliamentary circles. This was the side of his own mind which Conrad muted in his fiction through the English accents of his narrators—Marlow, the professor of languages, and the seaman who recalls the voyage of the "Narcissus." It was the part of Conrad's mind that the English called morbid[4] because it preferred resistance and death to compromise in the face of overwhelming adversity. It was the side that defended fanaticism as the source of some of the noblest human passions as well as the most degrading. It was the side that yearned after "a fixed standard of conduct" that could be recognized universally, and thought that doubt in such a standard was of man's creation.

But to seek out the "political Conrad" is by no means to suggest that Conrad, the novelist, wrote as a Polish partisan, or any other kind of partisan. Even the months he spent smuggling arms from Marseilles to Spain in the service of the Carlists—a period for which we have little documentation beside Conrad's own glamorous but self-deprecating accounts, fictional and autobiographical—even these months seem to savor more of the fantasy from which books are made than of calculated political activity. The only case to be made is that accidents of national origin and family background compelled him from earliest childhood to see in life a political dimension that strongly affected his perspective of all human affairs.

Many of Conrad's least political works convey to us the psychopolitical image of men bent on sailing to utopia but turned back by disaster, futility, or both. In *The Nigger of the "Narcissus,"* the ship is a "little world" that

> went on its curved and unswerving path carrying a discontented and aspiring population. They found comfort of a gloomy kind in an interminable and conscientious analysis of their unappreciated worth; and inspired by Donkin's hopeful doctrines they dreamed enthusiastically of the time when every lonely ship would travel over a serene sea, manned by a wealthy and well-fed crew of satisfied skippers.[5]

And in "Youth" the aging Marlow recalls how once, in fantasy, he had been able to transcend the pattern of existence which the voyage of the

[4]See Author's Note in *Lord Jim*, further discussed in Chap. ii. All references to Conrad's works are to the Collected Edition (London: Dent, 1946–55), unless otherwise specified.

[5]*The Nigger of the "Narcissus,"* p. 103.

"Judea" symbolized, one of those voyages that seem "an illustration of life," where you

> fight, work, sweat, nearly kill yourself, sometimes do kill yourself, trying to accomplish something—and you can't. Not from any fault of yours. You simply can do nothing, neither great nor little—not a thing in the world—not even marry an old maid, or get a wretched 600-ton cargo of coal to its port of destination.[6]

England had no recent experience of this kind of "voyage" when Conrad made his home there. She knew only the peace of the *pax Britannica,* a peace rooted in her policy of delicately balancing one hostile power against another, of avoiding challenges to any power on a hard basis of right and wrong. Even today, wherever one finds a Polish colony, one will hear the peculiar Polish defense of British freedom mixed with resentment of Britain's methods of maintaining it—methods which persistently refused official recognition of Polish right against Russian might.[7]

If Conrad had a maturing effect on English letters, it was in part because he called attention to the sheer horror in certain political realities that were being overlooked by comfortable, loaw-abiding English citizens and politicians. A sense of impending disaster, probably found in childhood memories, seems to have been as ingrained in Conrad's temperament, as it was in that of Lord Jim, who had no such childhood experience. (Hence, perhaps, Conrad's inability to understand why Jim's sensitivities baffled many English readers.) Conrad's early life, as seen through his uncle's letters particularly, makes us wonder to what extent his chronic drift toward reverie may have caused his fear of emergency situations—his fear that he would go blind like Captain Whalley, for instance[8]—and to what extent the tendency to dream was itself caused by early experiences of disaster.

At any rate, Conrad seems to have distrusted in himself the "morbid excess" that Coleridge named in Hamlet: the loss of "*equilibrium* between the real and the imaginary worlds," as a result of which "the

---

[6]*Youth,* p. 4.

[7]For an interesting study of the episode when Lord Palmerstone inconclusively attempted to send aid to the Polish insurrectionists of Apollo Korzeniowski's fatal rebellion, see W. E. Mosse, "England and the Polish Insurrection of 1863," *English Historical Review,* January 1956, pp. 28–55.

[8]". . . the story of the captain who went blind in 'The End of the Tether' had its source, according to Captain Craig, in Conrad's fears for his own eyes aboard the 'Vidar.' " G. Jean-Aubry, *La Vie de Conrad,* translated by Helen Sebba as *The Sea Dreamer* (New York: Doubleday, 1957), p. 239.

images of his fancy are far more vivid than his actual perceptions."[9] A line might be traced from Hamlet through Conrad to Lord Jim, suggesting the intimate alliance between political necessity and imaginative flight in men with a keen sense of responsibility to their social commitments.

While trying to relate Conrad's political thinking to the politics of his time, one keeps meeting a curious riddle: Why is a Polish émigré like an English Tory? Those who think first of Conrad's nostalgia for lost legitimacies in the courts of Europe (specifically in Spain and France) brand him a Conservative, failing to note that the main attraction of these royalist causes was not that they were legitimate but that they were (like the Polish cause) lost. No one of the English parties favored the ideals of government in Conrad's mind. As his son John reports,[10] he was never known to vote in an English election in the thirty-eight years of his British citizenship. He was born, and remained, "a man without a country." The nation that existed only in his mind was wonderful indeed, for it was governed without having a government. The abolished constitution of the old Polish Republic remained for him, as it had for his father, both vague and correct, a marvelous paradox of freedom and control as eternally mirrored in "the Polish temperament":

> Nothing is more foreign than what in the literary world is called Slavonism to the Polish temperament with its tradition of self-government, its chivalrous view of moral restraints and an exaggerated respect for individual rights: not to mention the important fact that the whole Polish mentality, Western in complexion, had received its training from Italy and France and, historically, had always remained, even in religious matters, in sympathy with the most liberal currents of European thought.[11]

To suggest that Conrad's political philosophy was based upon a never-never land and not conceived for practical purposes might be to discourage some readers from further inquiry into the political aspects of his fiction. Because it was detached perforce, however, from the patriotism that Samuel Johnson called "the last refuge of a scoundrel," Conrad's mind had the advantage of greater freedom in criticizing the actual and imagining the unattained. What he lost through the impossibility of direct action he may have gained in the heightened reality he

[9]Samuel Taylor Coleridge, "Hamlet," *The Complete Works,* IV, ed. W. G. I. Shedd (New York: Harper & Bros., 1884), p. 145.

[10]Interview with John Conrad, Canterbury (England), June 17, 1956.

[11]*A Personal Record,* pp. vi–vii.

found in his reading and the imaginative power with which he imbued his limited political experience. "No one has *known*—for intellectual use—the things you know," Henry James wrote him in 1906; ". . . you have, as the artist of the whole matter, an authority that no one has approached."[12]

Conrad's stature as a novelist is apparent to us, however little we may be aware of it, by the immense range of his perceptions and interests. He neither neglects nor belittles anything of importance on the human stage. He outdistances novelists like Ford Madox Ford, Virginia Woolf, and E. M. Forster, who sometimes wrote on the same themes he chose and were often more adroit technicians and more appealing storytellers, by his continued application to the whole human story and his resulting humility as a writer within it. His ambition as a writer was appalling if one thinks of it: ". . . literary creation being only one of the legitimate forms of human activity has no value but on the condition of not excluding the *fullest recognition to all the more distinct forms of action.*"[13]

Politics, surely the most distinct and comprehensive form of human action, has for Conrad a broader applicability than for many English-writing novelists of the last century. And yet we find politics treated in a purer form in *Nostromo, The Secret Agent,* and *Under Western Eyes* than in many novels which are now coming to be classed as political. Conrad's characters and incidents, with rare exceptions, recurrently open a double perspective into their private and public significance. For this reason, even such novels as *The Nigger of the "Narcissus," Lord Jim,* and *The Secret Sharer* bear the impress of the politically engaged Conrad. Nearly all his principal characters fall into situations where their personal action or thought is challenged by public forces with which they are incompatible and with which they must be reconciled. Justice, which for Plato and Aristotle was the aim of all political controversy, is the objective toward which his characters tend. And they end, like Lord Jim and Razumov, by giving up the struggle for their private causes and standing for judgment before the common conscience of their readers, which their trials have helped to enlighten.

If we consider two of the most readable books written in recent years on the subject of the political novel, we discover that no category has been made to accommodate Conrad. Morris Speare's *The Political Novel, Its Development in England and America*[14] limits itself almost

---

[12]Letter to Conrad, Nov. 1, 1906, in *Selected Letters of Henry James,* ed. Leon Edel (New York: Farrar, Straus and Cudahy, 1955), p. 157.

[13]"Books," *Notes on Life and Letters,* p. 7. The italics are mine.

[14]Morris Edmund Speare. *The Political Novel: Its Development in England and America* (New York: Oxford University Press, 1924).

entirely to novels that center on Parliament or Congress. Irving Howe's provocative *Politics and the Novel*[15] skilfully evades any definition of politics at all, but the introductory essay is crucial. Howe points out that, in the nineteenth century, the political novel developed when the novelist's attention was forced away from "the luxury of being able to take society for granted" and "had necessarily to shift from the gradations within society to the fate of society itself." At this point, "the idea of society, as distinct from the mere unquestioned workings of society, has penetrated the consciousness of the characters in all of its profoundly problematic aspects. . . ."[16]

I do not think it would be an annoying quibble to ask a question that Howe omits to consider. Can we discuss the general subject of politics—"the idea of society"—in the novel without establishing at least a tentative definition of what we mean by politics, or even what we mean by society? Perhaps prudently, Howe prefers to let his readers infer the meanings of these words (which may be many) from his discussion of the individual novelists. Yet through his essays one grows increasingly aware that the critic's definitions inevitably refract the light he throws upon his subjects. Howe's own genuine political concern appears to reflect the opinion most common to American political novelists—Hawthorne, James, Faulkner, Robert Penn Warren, and others who are such good bait for his hook—that politics, regardless of its origins, is a soul-sullying or at best a tragic business. This point of attack may serve our reading of American novelists, but it will not do for Conrad, whose idealism, though ultimately not much hardier than the Americans', leads him again and again to sympathetic consideration of the positive bases of government in human nature.

Howe finally looks on politics, in negative terms chiefly, "as both temptation and impediment," and he singles out the main characteristic of the political novel as a turn towards "apolitical temptation." Thus he rates Conrad below Dostoevsky as a political novelist by reading in the message of *Nostromo* and *Under Western Eyes* an ultimate retreat from political engagement to "the resources of private affection and gentleness."[17]

The alternation Howe examines between the political novelist's imaginative engagement in a historic cause and subsequent retreat to a pastoral celebration of private life (which may have been sacrificed in the political struggle) need not always be a veering between opposites. For Conrad particularly, every individual life contains the elements of commitment and withdrawal that characterize the political dilemma.

[15]Irving Howe, *Politics and the Novel* (New York: Horizon Press, 1957).
[16]*Ibid.*, p. 19.
[17]*Ibid.*, p. 23.

Indeed, his much-discussed preoccupation with human isolation is both cause and result of his strong sense of man's necessary involvement in social effort.

Man cannot retire. Conrad does not dream poetically, as did Boris Pasternak, of a society in which retirement is possible. Politics is implicit in the ego. Man is a political animal for Conrad as much as for Plato and Aristotle, whose writings he knew directly or indirectly through his Catholic background or his school reading.[18] "There must be a union of those who cannot exist without each other," Aristotle reasoned, and the necessary association of families must finally lead to establishment of "a single complete community, large enough to be nearly or quite self-sufficing." At this point, said Aristotle, the state comes into existence, "originating in the bare needs of life, and continuing in existence for the sake of a good life."[19]

This fundamental definition of politics is implicit in Conrad's writing but comes through his novels carrying the terrible burdens modern history has placed upon it. "The good life" (the main theme of the pastoral convention, incidentally) for which the state exists is a tragic fugitive in *Under Western Eyes,* symbolized specifically in a recurring image of winged youth. In *Nostromo* it is achieved at awful cost and built from faulty materials on the edge of a precipice.

Conrad makes difficulties for his readers—often unconsciously, sometimes deliberately, in such complex works as *Heart of Darkness* and *Nostromo*—by concentrating on the self-deceptions that lead virtuous men astray in their pursuit of the good life, which must be a life of public as well as private good. Whether these deceptions are inherent in human nature or result from the pride of Western civilization, whether they are part of the plan of creation or only the effect of unscrupulosity in man's thinking—these speculations crowd in upon the reader, throwing a dense foliage across the path of the story. The author finally seems to waver uncertainly between two possibilities and to conclude by leaving them in the form of a paradox that would doubtless have grated upon

[18]"While I was a boy in a great public school [in Austrian Cracow] we were steeped in classicism to the lips, and, though our historical studies were naturally tinted with Germanism, I know that all we boys, the six hundred of us, resisted that influence with all our might, while accepting the results of German research and thoroughness." Letter from Conrad to George T. Keating, Dec. 14, 1922, in *Life and Letters,* II, p. 289.

[19]Aristotle, *Politica,* translated by Benjamin Jowett, in *Introduction to Aristotle,* ed. Richard McKeon (New York: Random House, 1947), pp. 554–55.

Aristotle's argument epitomizes the more diffuse argument of Plato. But for Plato, unlike Aristotle, politics is less interesting as a study in itself than as an activity to be defined in seeking the nature of the ideal state, or of justice, which Plato finds only in a strict division of labor. See *The Republic of Plato,* translated by F. M. Cornford (Oxford: Oxford University Press, 1941), pp. 52–57.

the mind of the rationalist Aristotle. The possibility that man is fundamentally good, potentially able to achieve the social harmony he mentally projects, stands against the possibility that man is basically corrupt
and his utopian schemes "fairy tales" that create political miseries for
the unimaginative, who wish only to be left alone. Conrad's subtlety in
contemplating these alternatives may be inferred from the wildly different conclusions critics reach on some of his works—*Lord Jim*, for
example. This novel is typical of Conrad's best work, tending as it does
toward an insoluble paradox of human perfectibility within imperfec-
tion. Each star, each butterfly, each blade of grass, "the mighty Kos-
mos in perfect equilibrium produces—this," says the German Stein in
Lord Jim. By contrast, he adds, "Man is amazing, but he is not a
masterpiece."[20] But perfection, the reader may conclude on the final
page, is a dream of men like Jim, not of butterflies. For Stein, the
pursuit of illusion is the mark of the romantic, and the romantic is the
most fully realized man. There is something of Aristotle's philosophy of
perfectly realizable potentialities in Stein's reverie, but there is nothing
in Aristotle of Stein's quasi-Christian praise of human suffering as the
means of self-realization.

   As we shall see, from earliest childhood Conrad had good reason
for dramatizing an opposition between "romanticism" and "realism,"
politcally as well as personally. Furthermore, the shift he made from
eastern to western Europe during his maturing years gave him a view of
European politics from an objective vantage point superior to that of
Gulliver or the Chinese "Citizen of the World." For Conrad was at
once more deeply involved in the fate of the cosmopolitan community
and less deeply involved than Swift or Goldsmith in the specific national grievances that date their writings for later readers.

   This advantage for Conrad, one must add, is the source of another
difficulty for his readers. We are never sure of the exact position of the
mind reflecting behind the composition—whether it is, as it were, with
the English reader or against him; whether it presents its case for our
mutual sympathy and understanding or for our edification and im-
provement.

   At a critical moment in Conrad's writing life, when he had dropped
The Rescue to write *Heart of Darkness* and *Lord Jim*, his friend R. B.
Cunninghame Graham invited him to a pacifist meeting in London in
the spring of 1899 (about the same time as the Hague Peace Conference
of that year). Conrad's answer provides us with our most concise text on
his political point of view. It is especially interesting because it seems to
follow a train of thought that Conrad was pursuing in his fiction, and its

---

[20]*Lord Jim*, p. 208.

tone is unequivocal, registering a stern corrective to the British point of view from the profound experience of a foreigner. The voice throughout the letter is the voice of a travel-weary European realist, grimly set upon disenchanting his idealistic British friend. "I am simply in the seventh heaven to find you like the 'H. of D.' so far," he begins, referring to the first installment of *Heart of Darkness* that had appeared in the February, 1899, issue of *Blackwood's Magazine*.

> You bless me indeed. Mind you don't curse me by and bye for the very same thing. There are two more instalments in which the idea is so wrapped up in secondary notions that you, even you!—may miss it. And also you must remember that I don't start with an abstract notion. I start with definite images and as their rendering is true some little effect is produced. So far the note struck chimes in with your convictions,— *mais après*. There is an *après*. But I think that if you look a little into the episodes, you will find in them the right intention, though I fear nothing that is practically effective.[21]

At once Conrad has fixed the lines of the argument. Definite images, truly rendered—this is the only effective artistic technique. Cunninghame Graham will agree to this, but there is more in *Heart of Darkness* than art. Conrad goes on to say that in politics, too, if the terms of argument are indefinite and untrue to life, all effect is lost. Practical effectiveness is the thing to try for. He fears that his efforts in this direction in *Heart of Darkness* are futile.

From the start of the letter Conrad lapses into French to warn his correspondent of a non-British emphasis. French is, among other things, the traditional language of mediation between England and the continent.

Cunninghame Graham is going to talk at the peace conference, and Conrad writes,

> If you want me to come I want still more to hear you. But I am not a peace man, not a democrat (I don't know what the word means really). . . . I can't be an accomplice after or before the fact to any sort of fraternity that includes the westerness [?] whom I so dislike.

The word "westerness," thus transcribed by Jean-Aubry with a question mark, is in the manuscript at Yale obviously "westerners" (*zapadniki*), a term in the political vocabulary of Russia which at that time referred to an assortment of Russians who sympathized with western European traditions. Peter Chaadaev and Paul Milukov were among

---

[21]Letter to Cunninghame Graham, Feb. 8, 1899, *Life and Letters,* I, pp. 268–70.

their best known apologists. The word had this specific application, though Conrad might have used it also for the Americans, second only to the Russians in his contempt at that period, for reasons that will appear. He goes on to say,

> I cannot admit the idea of fraternity, not so much because I believe it impracticable, but because its propaganda (the only thing really tangible about it) tends to weaken the national sentiment, the preservation of which is my concern.

International brotherhood, Conrad stresses, is not a valid political aim.[22] Even if it could be, its profession at this moment is a dangerous red herring that will be used by malicious forces to fool and finally trample the credulous within free nations. The "illusion" of international fraternity "imposes by its size alone":

> There is already as much fraternity as there can be,—and that's very little and that very little is no good. What does fraternity mean? Abnegation,—self-sacrifice means something. Fraternity means nothing unless the Cain-Abel business. That's your true fraternity. *Assez*.

There is more to this fragile cynicism than at first meets the eye. Conrad is in effect hardly less sanguine politically than was Aristotle, for whom the basis of politics was not in brotherhood (an abstraction) but in a pragmatic "union of those who cannot exist without each other." Aristotle (again following Plato), while appealing to the far-reaching principle that the whole (in this case society) must have priority over the part, nonetheless set a limitation upon the size of societies, determining them not by the whole race of men but by integrations formed for efficiency: communities "large enough to be nearly or quite self-sufficing."[23] For Conrad, especially the Conrad of *Heart of Darkness,* efficiency is an inadequate criterion for the determination of size in a national state. With good reason, too, since one time-honored justification presented by Russia for her annexations of Polish territory was, and has continued to be, on the basis of a politically efficient union

[22]Some six years later, in 1905, Conrad writes that the beginnings of European fraternity were squelched by the Franco-Prussian War: "The idea of a Europe united in the solidarity of her dynasties, which for a moment seemed to dawn on the horizon of the Vienna Congress through the subsiding dust of Napoleonic alarums and excursions, has been extinguished by the larger glamour of less restraining ideals. Instead of the doctrines of solidarity it was the doctrine of nationalities much more favorable to spoliations that came to the front, and since its greatest triumphs at Sadowa and Sedan there is no Europe." *Notes on Life and Letters,* p. 103.

[23]Aristotle, *op. cit.,* p. 555.

of lands and peoples. In the letter to Cunninghame Graham Conrad
speaks for the first time to a British subject out of the depths of his
Polish political background. He has risen to defend not Poland but
nationalism—"national sentiment, the preservation of which is my
concern."

The national state, suffering persecution in the name of internationalism and brotherhood among other things, is an established fact.
Conrad makes no effort to defend it except on the strength of its concrete existence. *"Il faut un principe défini,"* he writes in the French
half of the letter in which his positive ideology is expressed.

> Si l'idée nationale apporte la souffrance et son service donne la mort, ça
> vaut toujours mieux que de servir les ombres d'une éloquence qui est
> morte, justement parce qu'elle n'a pas de corps.

Although this is the extent of his apology for the nation state, more
can be inferred from what is really the crux of the whole letter and,
significantly, the turning point at which Conrad lapses completely into
French, a language of clear definitions. The crucial term *"l'égoïsme"*
which he poses against the English "fraternity" is made to suggest not
only the care for self that sets man against his brother, but also the care
for the nation, which has set him, Conrad, against "international fraternity." His childhood exposure to German (antiromantic) historiography
may well have led to an interest in the historical works of Hegel and
Nietzsche and fortified a Polish romantic tendency toward identification
of the nation with the self.[24] For Hegel, and for Nietzsche after him, the
nation represented the highest expression of human destiny in man's
progress toward self-realization and perfect freedom. The clashes of
nation against nation, far from tending toward an international synthesis
as in Marx, would produce (according to Hegel and Nietzsche) an ever
increasing refinement of national spirit and a breed of supermen to
defend it. Conrad was deprecating in his references to these German
historians,[25] but their tracks are evident in his political fiction. The
evidence in the letter to Cunninghame Graham is to be inferred only
from the circumstance of his pairing egoism and nationalism against
fraternity and internationalism. Typically, Conrad restyles whatever he
may derive from political idealists into personal convictions edged with

[24]See above, n. 18.
[25]"The Germanic Tribes had told the whole world in all possible tones carrying conviction, the gently persuasive, the coldly logical; in tones Hegelian, Nietzschean, war-like,
pious, cynical, inspired, what they were going to do to the inferior races of the earth, so
full of sin and unworthiness." "The Crime of Partition" in *Notes on Life and Letters,* pp.
124–25.

a wry realism. In the letter to Cunninghame Graham, his train of thought on egoism and nationalism leads him to consider the nature of man in its aspect of eternal perversity rather than its godlike potentialities. Human society has its origins, its present, and its future in the conflicts of human egoism, out of which comes everything that we hate, but also everything that we love:

> L'homme est un animal méchant. Sa méchanceté doit être organisée. La société est essentiellement criminelle,—ou elle n'existerait pas. C'est l'égoïsme qui sauve tout,—absolument tout,—tout ce que nous abhorrons, tout ce que nous aimons. Et tout se tient. Voilà pourquoi je respecte les extrêmes anarchistes.—'Je souhaite l'extermination générale.' Très bien. C'est juste et ce qui est plus, c'est clair. On fait des compromis avec des paroles. Ça n'en finit plus. C'est comme une forêt où personne ne connaît la route.

Between the lines we may read the experience of a man (and a people) whose past knowledge of anarchy and present knowledge of oppression have revealed not only the need for organized society but the need to dissolve it when it has been turned against him. Suppression, since 1772 (the first partition of Poland), has discovered to him his formerly unexploited powers for rebellion.

But the urge back to anarchy sits uneasily upon a people who pride themselves upon a flair for political justice and stability (pride all the stronger because the old Polish Republic is beyond the test of practical politics). Their political cynicism, except as it is directed toward oppression, is consciously nurtured as a measure of self-defense and a refuge:

> C'est un égoïsme rationnel et féroce que j'exerce envers moi-même. Je me repose là-dedans. Puis la pensée revient. La vie recommence, les regrets, les souvenirs et un désespoir plus sombre que la nuit.

The political animal for Conrad has a dual nature, empowered with titanic good and titanic evil, as a result of which he is at war both with himself and with his fellow men. To the British Cunninghame Graham, Conrad writes as Thomas Hobbes wrote to the whole English nation, trying to waken it from a dream of utopias to the daylight of a Machiavellian *Realpolitik* that the continent had been digesting for over a century. Hobbes, too, probed into the egoism that is the motive force toward both criminal behavior and social good. But Hobbes, like many of his contemporaries, was bent on convincing his readers of something in which Conrad had no faith—the possibility of an empirical demonstration for all truth. Utilitarian democracy, the "enlightened self-interest" of Hobbes, Bentham, and Mill, as of the American Transcendentalists, is surely the "lovely phantom" of democracy which Conrad derides for his friend's benefit. Leashing its hope to a dream of material wealth like the English hero of *Nostromo,* this phantom has opened the way for a form of government that will force, rather than allow, men to have what they need. Over a decade earlier Conrad had written to Spiridion Kliszczewski that "England was the only barrier to the pressure of infernal doctrines born in continental back-slums." But as a result of an untimely extension of the suffrage, socialism was inevitable, he said, and "must inevitably end in Caesarism." "These things must be. It is a fatality."[26]

Finally, the egoism that asserts the inalienable truth of national existence for Conrad is no more like the egoism of Hobbes than it is like the egoism of Nietzsche. His resort to French is meaningful in another way here, I believe. Some seven years earlier he wrote in French to his relative Marguerite Poradowska of the same faculty for self-sacrifice that, in the letter to Cunninghame Graham, he holds to "mean something," having its source in egoism rather than brotherhood. To Madame Poradowska, a Frenchwoman married to a Pole, he traces "that mysterious urge toward abnegation and suffering which guides womanly feeling" back to its source in charity. "For Charity is eternal and universal Love, the divine virtue, the sole manifestation of the Almighty which may in some manner justify the act of creation.

"Hence the longing for self-sacrifice, for returing good for evil. . . ."[27] Words written to a woman, to a devout Roman Catholic, but the only words he gives anywhere for the origins of the urge toward heroism. And he adds, even to her, the essence of his message to Cunninghame Graham:

> Unfortunately . . . in my opinion abnegation carried to an extreme . . . is not only profoundly immoral but dangerous, in that it sharpens the appetite for evil in the malevolent and develops (perhaps unconsciously) that latent human tendency towards hypocrisy in the . . . let us say, benevolent.

The British socialist and the French Catholic bring out in Conrad two sides of the same thought. Sympathetic with both correspondents, he

---

[26]Letter to Kliszczewski, Dec. 19, 1885, *Life and Letters,* I, p. 84.

[27]*Letters of Joseph Conrad to Marguerite Poradowska, 1890–1920,* translated and edited by John A. Gee and Paul J. Sturm (New Haven: Yale University Press, 1940), p. 42.

yet corrects what he takes to be Cunninghame Graham's utopian conception of human nature and the foundations of society, and the Catholic woman's uncritical trust in benevolence.

But the English-speaking reader often mistakenly identifies Conrad's political dualism with arch-conservatism for want of understanding its Polish frame of reference, particularly in the letter to Cunninghame Graham. The difficult passage is the crucial *"l'homme est un animal méchant. Sa méchanceté doit être organisée. Le crime est une condition necéssaire de l'existence organisée. La société est essentiellement criminelle,—ou elle n'existerait pas."* To British and American readers, with their history of relative political security and slowly evolving democratic institutions, Conrad appears to stand "on the lunatic fringe of conservatism." Such is the opinion of one American reader, who then concludes: "The respect for tradition, for law, for convention, [was] a product of his belief that society arose not as a manifestation of similar qualities in individuals, and hence to be subordinate to them, but that it was imposed as a necessary restraint upon man's innate depravity."[28] The trouble with this is that *méchanceté* is not—as Jocelyn Baines, too, translates it in the concluding pages of his recent biography—"depravity" (a single quality—evil unqualified) but something better rendered as "perversity" (which is dual, implying a norm of goodness and a straying from it). This is, in fact, the common quality in all men of which organized society is the full manifestation. Society is thus formed not as an imposition upon evil human nature, but arises out of the expression of that nature, good and bad. Just as each man must organize his own perversity in order to live with himself, he and his fellows must organize one another's perversity so that they can all live together. Conrad lays a heavier onus upon organized society (*essentiellement criminelle*) than upon man (*méchant*). Man is lovable in his perversity, but organized society is a necessary evil. A strong satiric theme in *The Secret Agent* follows logically from this: The lawkeepers have the same criminal instincts as the lawbreakers, otherwise the whole legal apparatus would collapse (*n'existerait pas*). It takes two to make an argument, a thief to catch a thief.

Conrad's political thought is less like arch-conservatism than it is like the lunatic fringe of Polish liberalism,[29] characteristically jealous of the privilege of anarchy but conscientiously hopeful of preserving each man's rights against his neighbor.

---

[28]Henry Steele Commager, Jr., "The Problem of Evil in *Heart of Darkness*," Bowdoin Prize Essay, Harvard University, 1952, p. 7.

[29]Poles have long prided themselves on the early democratization of their political institutions, developed between the fourteenth and eighteenth centuries, before the abolition of the Polish Republic. Among their advances during this period were the grants of

Both the German submissiveness (idealistic as it may be) and the Russian lawlessness (fed on the corruption of all the virtues) are utterly foreign to the Polish nation, whose qualities and defects are altogether of another kind, tending to a certain exaggeration of individualism and, perhaps, to an extreme belief in the Governing Power of Free Assent: the one invariably vital principle in the internal government of the Old Republic.[30]

"C'est l'égoïsme qui sauve tout . . . tout ce que nous abhorrons, tout ce que nous aimons." An apt summary of Poland's experience with the *Liberum Veto,* which from 1652 (when it was first applied—it had been introduced earlier) till its abolition in 1791 gave each deputy of the Diet the right to defeat any resolution before the legislature by his single opposition. Out of this wild experiment in utopian democracy came not only the freedom Poland loved but the disunion that finally destroyed her. She was, nevertheless, heading toward a form of government that would reflect as fully as possible the demands of human nature.

The kind of order required by man should be congruent with his nature rather than contradictory to it. This is the essence of Conrad's message to Cunninghame Graham. Socialism, robbing men of natural incentives to self-government and inner moral restraint, leads on to "Caesarism." "Democracy," on the other hand, has corrupt connotations for Conrad because it is tainted with the abstractions that incited the French Revolution or the lawlessness of American bossism in the West, and in eastern Europe it is a mounting battle cry for revolutionary forces quickened by hatred for much that is good as well as much that is corrupt in Western civilization. Conrad distinguishes sharply between Cunninghame Graham's democratic instincts (in the letter: *"vous êtes essentiellement un frondeur. . . .C'est les nobles qui ont fait la Fronde, du reste,"*) and "that humanitarianism that seems to be merely a matter of crazy nerves or a morbid conscience."[31] In his novels,

---

personal inviolability by the king to the nobility in 1428, the institution of a parliamentary system (the Polish Diet) and constitutional monarchy in 1505, the invention of the veto power (*Liberum Veto,* 1652), and the extension of political rights to nearly 12 per cent of the whole population. By contrast, "the Liberal France of Louis-Philippe did not grant such rights to 1 per cent of her citizens. . . . In Great Britain, before the reform of 1832, less than 2 per cent of the inhabitants had the right to vote." The myth concerning Polish conservatism, many Poles believe, was created and popularized by German historians who labeled the Polish Republic an Aristocratic Oligarchy, without taking into account that the Polish aristocracy made up a small portion of the voting nobility. See *Poland,* An authorized version of *Petite Encyclopédie Polonaise,* ed. Erasmus Piltz (London, 1909), pp. 28–29 n. and pp. 389–416.

[30]"The Crime of Partition," *Notes on Life and Letters,* p. 132.

[31]*A Personal Record,* p. vii.

Charles Gould represents the former, Peter Ivanovitch and Donkin the latter.

In an unpublished portion of the manuscript of *Under Western Eyes*, which must be examined separately, Conrad hinted strongly at a tragic stalemate that could occur in world politics if Europe were to be caught between the two camps of Russian autocratic socialism and American commercial individualism.

Conrad wrote to Cunninghame Graham in the spring of 1899 from the standpoint of a Pole recalling with mingled pride and regret the long history of Polish liberal institutions which had sickened and finally died because Poland had plucked the fruit of democracy before it was ripe. He is in the peculiar position of a man (three generations removed from practical politics) whose inherited memory of it is yet so vivid that he feels justified in admonishing the inexperienced. His advice, furthermore, is not simply against the democracy in which Poland failed, but a subtle compound of faith and despair. It is the inexperience of his adopted English countrymen that calls forth his prophetic insights into modern politics.

John A. Palmer

"Achievement and Decline":
A Bibliographical Note

The idea of Conrad's achievement and decline was first developed at length in Douglas Hewitt's *Conrad: A Reassessment* (Cambridge: Bowes and Bowes, 1952), and received its chief impetus from Thomas Moser's *Joseph Conrad: Achievement and Decline* (Cambridge: Harvard University Press, 1957) and Albert J. Guerard's *Conrad the Novelist* (Cambridge: Harvard University Press, 1958). These valuable critical works have recently been buttressed by Bernard C. Meyer, M.D., *Joseph Conrad: A Psychoanalytic Biography* (Princeton: Princeton University Press, 1967). The notion had been suggested as early as 1927, however, in John Galsworthy's "Reminiscences of Conrad," in *Castles in Spain and Other Screeds* (New York: Scribners, 1927); and Vernon Young had anticipated most of the argument, including the Moser-Meyer analysis of Conrad's misogyny, in "Joseph Conrad: Outline for a Reconsideration," *Hudson Review* II:5–19 (Spring 1949).

Hewitt, who dates Conrad's decline from the end of 1909 (when he had just finished "The Secret Sharer"), believes that at that point Conrad "started to suppress those aspects of his sensibility which give value to such works as 'Heart of Darkness,' 'Falk,' *Nostromo, The Secret Agent,* 'The End of the Tether,' *Lord Jim* and 'The Secret Sharer.' It is strange that Conrad . . . should in the latter part of his life have written so much which obscures the valuable qualities of his early works. . . . I [have been] forced to the conclusion that, despite his conscious attention to his craft, he was—particularly after the deterioration set in—far less aware of his real powers than one would expect" (p. 4). In the later works Conrad represses his earlier high awareness of human complexity, and more specifically of "the darker side of even our good feelings"—an "evasion" which accounts for the "obvious flaws" in a novel like *Chance:* "its clichés, its defensive irony, its imprecise rhetoric" (p. 89), and so on. The later fiction is populated with characters who are either all good or all bad, and as a result is marred by a sentimental tone and melodramatic structure. Conrad's sense of evil returned to the depths with Leggatt, never to reappear in the same form: "There seems to have been within him a continual war between the recognition of the 'heart of darkness' and the desire to rest securely on unquestioned values. His letters tend to show that the desire for security was the more conscious, but in the best of the early works the 'other self' cannot be denied. . . . With 'The Secret Sharer' Conrad seems to resolve this conflict for his peace of mind, and we must now consider the works which follow it" (p. 79). Of all these later works, only *The Shadow-Line,* in Hewitt's view, is free "from all the flaws of lush rhetoric and moralizing which disfigure the others" (p. 112).

Moser's chief purpose is not so much to establish Conrad's decline (which he sees as beginning a little later, with *Chance* in 1912), as to explain it. To do this, he adds a psychoanalytic dimension to Hewitt's theory. At the same time that Conrad was "turning his back on moral judgment" (p. 130), Moser tells us, he was also devoting himself to a subject he secretly feared and therefore could not successfully dramatize—namely, love: "Conrad's decision to finish *Chance* determined his decline. In his early major period, he had, as we have seen, either evaded love or subordinated it to other subjects. *Chance* has love for its central subject, as do *Victory, The Arrow of Gold, The Rescue, The Rover,* and the unfinished *Suspense.* Of the later novels, only *The Shadow-Line* does not deal with love. Such a radical shift in subject naturally raises the unanswerable question: why? Why did Conrad cease those explorations into moral failure in the masculine world that had enabled him to achieve artistic success?" (p. 102). Besides sharing Hewitt's view of the moral tone and technique of the later works, Moser holds that "love," as it appears in these works, is essentially destructive: "The world is full of evil, except in certain characters whom Conrad likes," and the greatest good for these "figures of purity afflicted by an external evil" is to "lose themselves in a love that will blot out all awareness of the world and bring the semblance of death" (pp. 141, 143). Moser points to a variety of evidence in Conrad's fiction—the absence of children borne from his love affairs and marriages, the paucity of dramatic give-and-take between his lovers, the persistence of threatening imagery in his sexual scenes, and so on—to show that Conrad could not really face up to his subject.

Guerard accepts the broad outlines of the Hewitt-Moser view. But his chief purpose is to provide detailed readings of Conrad's best fiction; he therefore spends less time analyzing Conrad's failures, and his explanation of the "decline" is more cautious: "Is the uncongeniality of love as a subject, and Conrad's later determination to present it 'affirmatively,' the most important cause of his serious anticlimax, as Moser affirms? Perhaps. I should insist more than he does, however, on the understandable exhaustion following upon the astonishing creative labors of 1894–1903, on the turn to European settings and a more conventional realistic manner, above all on the effects of dictation. But I could not agree more warmly that the best work of Conrad is the work of a tragic pessimist, concerned with other kinds of masculine failure than sexual" (p. 55). Like other readers who find an achievement and decline in Conrad, Guerard objects to the apparent lack of psychological and moral complexity in his later work; and he finds the later style too rhetorical, too sentimental, and too often faulty in syntax and grammar—characteristics which, along with the relative frequency of Gallicisms in the later prose, are taken as evidence of Conrad's flagging energies.

Meyer's volume is the final product of a series of articles in psychiatric and literary journals; quite understandably, it supersedes Moser's as a psychoanalytic study; and it is unquestionably one of the most valuable biographical sources on Conrad. Conrad's artistic decline, according to Meyer, was brought about "not by physical ill health, mental fatigue, or financial worries, not by the necessity to dictate his novels, not by his 'relative isolation' or other environmental factors, but rather by the inevitable consequence of the specific psychological defenses adopted by him after his mental illness [in 1910]." No longer able to afford those "introspective journeys into the self" that had characterized the best of his earlier work, Conrad elected to "confine his art to the surface of life," willfully cutting himself off from "the dream source of poetic invention" and "the rich lode of his own well-guarded fancy" (p. 243). Meyer's evidence for these assertions, and for his broader theories about the conflicts and fetishes that "played a crucial role in facilitating or diminishing the fullest expression" of Conrad's gift (p. 14), is detailed and impressive. But having started with Moser, Guerard, and Frederick Karl (another achievement-and-decline critic) as his literary authorities, Meyer accepts the "patent deterioration of [Conrad's] artistry during the second half of his literary career" (p. 4) as a *donnée,* thus foreclosing the essential critical question from the beginning.

Within these broad areas of agreement, certain specific value judgments have also come to be shared by achievement-and-decline critics—the greatness of "Heart of Darkness" and *Nostromo,* for example, or the near-total failure of *The Arrow of Gold. Victory,* since it has traditionally been viewed as the best of Conrad's later novels, is a crucial case. "It would be tempting to pass over it in silence," Guerard says, "could one only be sure that readers would eventually reach the excellent critiques of Douglas Hewitt and Thomas Moser. For this is one of the worst novels for which high claims have ever been made by critics of standing: an awkward popular romance built around certain imperfectly dramatized reflections on skepticism, withdrawal, isolation," and including story elements appealing chiefly to the "adolescent" mind—the "rudimentary but exciting adventure story, the romantic pose of world-weary detachment, the simple yet vague erotic fantasy of the island shared with a grateful uneducated girl." Like Hewitt and Moser, Guerard objects to the novel's shifting point of view, its implausibly rhetorical dialogue, "flat and unenergized" prose, and "sentimentality and vagueness," and believes that "the time has come to drop *Victory* from the Conrad canon" (pp. 272 ff.)—a judgment since echoed by other influential critics (e.g., David Daiches, *New York Times* Book Review, August 17, 1958, p. 4; R. W. Stallman, "Conrad Criticism Today," *Sewanee Review* LXVII:137 [Winter 1959]). Similarly, it is fashionable among achievement-and-decline critics to reject Conrad's later letters and prefaces as clues to his art, especially where they are in the reductive vein of the "few very simple ideas" passage. Hewitt holds that to read the early works in the light of the prefaces would be "to miss almost everything which they have to give us" (p. 4); but on matters of artistic method Conrad may be trusted: "Though . . . Conrad often seems to misunderstand the nature of the issues with which his early work deals, his more specifically technical comments are far more acute and reliable" (p. 6). According to Frederick Karl, the Author's Notes are "docile," rooted in fact instead of imagination, and show the same decline of conceptual power as the later fiction (*A Reader's Guide to Joseph Conrad* [New York: Noonday Press, 1960], p. 41). In its extreme form, the idea that Conrad's self-criticism is misleading becomes a charge of coyness or dishonesty: Conrad's declaration that "I did not wrap [*Victory*] up in very mysterious processes of art" is, Stallman says, "nothing less than a strategic feint to conceal the secret intentions of *Victory*, and it is characteristic of that cunning strategy by which he everywhere conceals what his books are really about" ("Conrad and 'The Secret Sharer,' " *Accent* IX:132 [Spring 1949]); Conrad's "disclosures about his literary aims are highly deceptive, often deliberately misleading," and his Author's Notes are planted with "bogus trade secrets" and "false clues" (pp. 135, 136). Meyer, taking it for granted that Conrad's later self-criticism is simplistic and self-deprecatory, views it as one more of Conrad's postpsychotic defenses against complexity, thus avoiding Stallman's moralistic tone, but reinforcing the essential point.

Some mutterings against the tyranny of "achievement and decline" have recently been heard in the journals; *Victory*, in particular, coming in for some sympathetic reassessment. . . . The idea that his career can profitably be viewed as growth within a fixed frame of reference, for example, is Conrad's own: "My writing life extends . . . over twenty-three years . . . and all that time has been a time of evolution. . . . Some critics have found fault with me for not being constantly myself. But they are wrong. . . . Certain conclusions remain immovably fixed in my mind, but . . . my attitude to subjects and expressions, the angles of vision, my methods of composition will, within limits, be always changing—not because I am unstable or unprincipled but because I am free" (*Life and Letters,* II, p. 204). Similarly, as Zabel has pointed out, the idea that his growth is not merely technical, but is part of a growing self-awareness, is Conrad's also: "The letters he wrote Mme. Poradowska between 1890 and 1900 reveal . . . [that] he was already groping for the means and courage to translate [his] experiences into fictional form, to objectify them dramatically, and thus to come into an intelligent realization of their meaning: to save himself, as he once expressed it, 'from the madness which, after a certain point in life is reached, awaits those who refuse to master their sensations and bring into coherent form the mysteries of their lives' " (Morton Dauwen Zabel, "Joseph Conrad: Chance and Recognition," *Sewanne Review* LIII [Winter 1945], as revised for his *Craft and Character in Modern Fiction* [New York: The Viking Press, 1957], p. 158). It has frequently been observed how insistently Conrad referred to the moral center of his work, but the point is worth repeating once again, since it has been the tendency of recent critics to ignore it: "I think I've got the theme for a Mediterranean novel with historical interest, intrigue and adventure. . . . All I want now is to discover the moral pivot"; or again, "I have been called a writer of the sea, of the tropics, a descriptive writer, a romantic writer—and also a realist. But as a matter of fact all my concern has been with the 'ideal' value of things, events and people. That and nothing else. The humorous, the pathetic, the passionate, the sentimental *aspects* came in of themselves—*mais en vérité c'est les valeurs idéales des faits et gestes humains qui se sont imposés à mon activité artistique" (Life and Letters,* II, pp. 42, 185). And in line with the development of his later fiction, Conrad's later letters display more frequent literary allusions, more frequent philosophical and political disquisitions, more frequent expressions of a refined skepticism, and the like. Disregarding its rather elegant theses, Edward W. Said's *Joseph Conrad and the Fiction of Autobiography* (Cambridge: Harvard University Press, 1966) furnishes some support for this point, arguing that the letters are "Conrad's spiritual history as written by Conrad himself" (p. 5), and that "the intellectual and spiritual climax of the letters . . . coincided not only with the fulfillment of his desire for self-discovery, but also with . . . the period of World War One" (pp. vi–vii), which is to say, the period of *Victory.*

The bias of early writers like Aubry and Mégroz toward biography and "personality" helped them to observe the ethical coherence of Conrad's work; but beyond that they see very little of Conrad's artistic growth. Muriel Bradbook's brief *Joseph Conrad: Poland's English Genius* (Cambridge: At the University Press, 1941), divides Conrad's work into three stages: "The Wonders of the Deep," from *Almayer's Folly* through the *Typhoon* volume; "The Hollow Men," from *Nostromo* through *Victory;* and "Recollections in Tranquility" for all the work after *Victory.* More valuable than these categories, perhaps, is her awareness of the growing technical complexity of Conrad's work, and of the near-allegorical quality of *Victory,* which she singles out, along with *The Rover,* for special praise. More recently, Paul L. Wiley's *Conrad's Measure of Man* (Madison: University of Wisconsin Press, 1954) has offered another tripartite view of Conrad's career, according to the central protagonist of each period: "Man in the World," "Man in Society," and "Man in Eden." Wiley's archetypal frame of reference and his too-vigorous pursuit of literary and intellectual relationships between Conrad and his contemporaries introduce some distortions; and he agrees with achievement-and-decline critics that romantic love is a matter of central concern in the later fiction. But there is considerable validity in his broad divisions of Conrad's career; and his inclination to resist the idea of a "decline" in Conrad, and to defend the later works against severe negative criticism, is of course shared by the present study. Of all the critics who have offered general descriptions of Conrad's career, however, the most stimulating may be

Zabel, whose "Chance and Recognition" and introductions to individual volumes are standard reading for students of Conrad. The commitment to human solidarity, Zabel says, is for Conrad "a necessity which defines man as human, his moral consciousness as imperative, and his persistence in that consciousness as the fundamental law of life. From this germinal presentation of the case Conrad's drama of the self widens until, in his most ambitious books, it comes to include the larger workings of that law in society and politics, even in the destiny of nations and of races. The growth in his thought from an idealistic conception of life to a critical one, from his temperamental romanticism to his later realism of values, is the drama of his genius in its difficult emergence." ("Chance and Recognition," as revised for *Craft and Character,* p. 166.) The idea that Conrad's career may be seen as an outward growth from a germinal center, toward the periphery of his intellectual vision and a more-and-more ambitious subject matter, is the theoretical spine of this book. And to see the conscious center of Conrad in an ethical view of the universe and of man's place in it, and the growth of his art as a progress in self-discovery—these points are crucial.

Selected Bibliography

NOVELS AND SHORT STORIES

Almayer's Folly, 1895.

An Outcast of the Islands, 1896.

The Nigger of the "Narcissus," 1897. Published in the United States as *Children of the Sea: A Tale of the Forecastle*.

Tales of Unrest, 1898. (Contents: "The Idiots," 1896; "Karain," 1897; "The Lagoon," 1897; "An Outpost of Progress," 1897; "The Return.")

Lord Jim, A Tale, 1900.

The Inheritors, An Extravagant Story, With Ford Madox Hueffer, 1901.

Youth, A Narrative, and Two Other Stories, 1902. Contents: "Youth," 1898; "Heart of Darkness," 1899; "The End of the Tether," 1902.)

Typhoon, 1902.

Typhoon and Other Stories, 1903. (Contents: "Amy Foster," 1901; "Typhoon," 1902; "To-Morrow," 1902; "Falk," 1903.)

Romance, A Novel. With Ford Madox Hueffer, 1903.

Nostromo, A Tale of the Seaboard, 1904.

The Secret Agent, A Simple Tale, 1907.

A Set of Six, 1908. (Contents: "An Anarchist," 1906; "The Brute," 1906; "Gaspar Ruiz," 1906; "The Informer," 1906; "The Duel," 1908; "Il Conde," 1908.)

Under Western Eyes, A Novel, 1911.

'Twixt Land and Sea, Tales, 1912. (Contents: "The Secret Sharer," 1910; "A Smile of Fortune," 1911; "Freya of the Seven Isles," 1912.)

Chance, A Tale in Two Parts, 1913.
Victory, An Island Tale, 1915.
Within the Tides, 1915. (Contents: "The Partner," 1911; "The Inn of the Two Witches," 1913; "Because of the Dollars," 1914; "The Planter of Malata," 1914.)
The Shadow-Line, A Confession, 1917.
The Arrow of Gold, A Story Between Two Notes, 1919.
The Rescue: A Romance of the Shallows, 1920.
The Rover, 1923.
The Nature of a Crime, With Ford Madox Hueffer, 1924.
Suspense, A Napoleonic Novel, 1925.
Tales of Hearsay, 1925. (Contents: "The Black Mate," 1908; "Prince Roman," 1911; "The Tale," 1917; "The Warrior's Soul." 1917.)
The Sisters, 1928.

ESSAYS AND REMINISCENCES

The Mirror of the Sea, Memories and Impressions, 1906.
A Personal Record. Also known as *Some Reminiscences,* 1908, 1912.
Notes on Life and Letters, 1921.
Last Essays, 1926.

DRAMATIC WORKS

One Day More, A Play in One Act, 1913. (Adaptation of "To-Morrow.")
The Secret Agent, Drama in Four Acts, 1921. (Adaptation of the novel.)
Laughing Anne, A Play, 1923. (Adaptation of "Because of the Dollars.")

LETTERS

Five Letters by Joseph Conrad to Edward Noble in 1895. London: Privately printed, 1925.

Joseph Conrad's Letters to His Wife. London: Privately printed, 1927.

Joseph Conrad: Life and Letters. Edited by G. Jean-Aubry. 2 vols. Garden City, N.Y.: Doubleday, 1927.

Conrad to a Friend, 150 Selected Letters from Joseph Conrad to Richard Curle. Edited by Richard Curle. New York: Crosby, Gaige, 1928.

Letters from Joseph Conrad, 1895–1924. Edited by Edward Garnett. Indianapolis: Bobbs-Merrill, 1928.

Lettres françaises. Edited by G. Jean-Aubry. Paris: Gallimard, 1929.

Letters of Joseph Conrad to Marguerite Poradowska, 1890–1920. Edited by John A. Gee and Paul J. Sturm. New Haven: Yale University Press, 1940. (Published in French in Geneva, Switzerland by Libraire Droz, René Rapin, ed., 1966.)

Joseph Conrad: Letters to William Blackwood and David S. Meldrum. Edited by William Blackburn. Durham, N.C.: Duke University Press, 1958.

Conrad's Polish Background: Letters to and from Polish Friends. Edited by Zdzisław Najder. London: Oxford University Press, 1964.

Joseph Conrad and Warrington Dawson: The Record of a Friendship. Edited by Dale B. J. Randall. Durham, N.C.: Duke University Press, 1968.

Joseph Conrad's Letters to Cunninghame Graham. Edited by C. T. Watts. Cambridge: At the University Press, 1969.

(Frederick R. Karl and Zdzisław Najder are co-editing Conrad's collected correspondence for publication in ten volumes, with the first two volumes scheduled to appear in 1975–76.)

COLLECTED EDITIONS

The Works of Joseph Conrad. 20 vols. London: Heinemann, 1921–27.

The Works of Joseph Conrad. The Uniform Edition. 22 vols. London: Dent, 1923–28.

Collected Works of Joseph Conrad. The Memorial Edition (later the Kent, Concord, Canterbury Editions). 21 vols. Garden City, N.Y.: Doubleday, Page, 1926. (*The Collected Edition of the Works of Joseph Conrad*, published in London by Dent in 1946–55, in 21 vols., was reprinted from the Uniform Edition, omitting the dramatic works.)

BIBLIOGRAPHIES

Kenneth A. Lohf and Eugene P. Sheehy, eds. *Joseph Conrad at Mid-Century: Editions and Studies 1895–1955.* Minneapolis: University of Minnesota Press, 1957.

Theodore G. Ehrsam, ed. *A Bibliography of Joseph Conrad.* Metuchen, N.J.: Scarecrow Press, 1969.

Bruce E. Teets and Helmut E. Gerber, eds. *Joseph Conrad: An Annotated Bibliography of Writings About Him.* DeKalb, Ill.: Northern Illinois University Press, 1971.

Modern Fiction Studies. February 1955 and Spring 1964. Selected bibliographies.

SELECTED WRITINGS ABOUT CONRAD
(An asterisk indicates an important work.)

Allen, Jerry. *The Sea Years of Joseph Conrad.* New York: Doubleday, 1965.

*Baines, Jocelyn. *Joseph Conrad.* New York: McGraw-Hill, 1960.

Bradbrook, M.C. *Joseph Conrad: Poland's English Genius.* Cambridge: At the University Press, 1941.

Conrad, Jessie [Mrs. Joseph]. *Joseph Conrad and His Circle.* New York: Dutton, 1935.

————. *Joseph Conrad: As I Knew Him.* Garden City, N.Y.: Doubleday, 1926.

"Conrad Supplement," *Transatlantic Review* II (3): 454–465, 570–582, 689–700 (August 1924).

Crankshaw, Edward. *Joseph Conrad: Some Aspects of the Art of the Novel.* London: John Lane, 1936.

Curle, Richard. *Joseph Conrad: A Study.* London: Kegan, Paul, Trench, Trubner, 1914. (The first book-length study.)

Dowden, Wilfred S. *"Almayer's Folly and Lord Jim:* A Study in the Development of Conrad's Imagery." *Rice University Studies* LI: 13–27 (Winter 1965).

————. "The 'Illuminating Quality': Imagery and Theme in *The Secret Agent.*" *Rice Institute Pamphlets* XLVII:17–33 (October 1960).

Fleishman, Avrom. *Conrad's Politics: Community and Anarchy in the Fiction of Joseph Conrad.* Baltimore: Johns Hopkins Press, 1967.

Ford, Ford Madox. *Joseph Conrad: A Personal Remembrance.* Boston: Little Brown, 1924. (Insights into Conrad's novelistic techniques.)

*Gordan, John Dozier. *Joseph Conrad: The Making of a Novelist.* Cambridge: Harvard University Press, 1941. (A classic of Conrad scholarship, especially for the early novels.)

*Guerard, Albert. *Conrad the Novelist.* Cambridge: Harvard University Press, 1958. (An important critical study of the major fiction.)

———. *Joseph Conrad.* New York: New Directions, 1947.

Guetti, James. " 'Heart of Darkness': The Failure of Imagination." In his *The Limits of Metaphor: A Study of Melville, Conrad, and Faulkner.* Ithaca: Cornell University Press, 1967.

Hay, Eloise Knapp. *The Political Novels of Joseph Conrad.* Chicago: University of Chicago Press, 1963.

Hewitt, Douglas. *Conrad: A Reassessment.* Cambridge, England: Bowes and Bowes, 1952. (A key interpreter of Conrad's decline in his last fifteen years.)

Howe, Irving. "Conrad: Order and Anarchy." In his *Politics and the Novel.* New York: Horizon Press, 1957. (An attack on Conrad's political sympathies.)

*Jean-Aubry, G. *Joseph Conrad: Life and Letters.* 2 vols. Garden City, N.Y.: Doubleday, 1927. (The first "full" account of Conrad's life and the source of many important letters.)

*Karl, Frederick R. *A Reader's Guide to Joseph Conrad.* New York: Farrar, Straus & Giroux, 1960; revised edition, 1969. (Discussions of all of Conrad's novels and stories.)

Kramer, Dale. "Marlow, Myth, and Structure in *Lord Jim.*" *Criticism* VIII:263–279 (Summer 1966).

Leavis, F. R. *The Great Tradition.* London: Chatto and Windus, 1948.

Lehmann, John, ed. *The London Magazine,* IV (11):21–49 (November 1957). (Essays on Conrad.)

*Meyer, Bernard. *Joseph Conrad: A Psychoanalytic Biography.* Princeton, N.J.: Princeton University Press, 1967.

Morf, Gustav. *The Polish Heritage of Joseph Conrad.* London: Sampson, Low, Marston, 1930.

Moser, Thomas. *Joseph Conrad: Achievement and Decline.* Cambridge: Harvard University Press, 1957.

*Najder, Zdzisław. *Conrad's Polish Background: Letters to and from Polish Friends.* London: Oxford University Press, 1964. (Important documentation of Conrad's Polish heritage.)

Perry, John Oliver. "Action, Vision, or Voice: The Moral Dilemmas in Conrad's Tale-Telling." *Modern Fiction Studies* X:3–14 (Spring 1964).

*Sherry, Norman. *Conrad's Eastern World*. Cambridge: At the University Press, 1966. (Solid documentation of Conrad's early sailing career and its influence on his fiction.)

————. *Conrad's Western World*. Cambridge: At the University Press, 1971.

Stallman, Robert Wooster. *The Art of Joseph Conrad: A Critical Symposium*. East Lansing: Michigan State University Press, 1960.

Tanner, Tony. "Butterflies and Beetles—Conrad's Two Truths." *Chicago Review* VI:123–140 (Winter-Spring 1963).

————. "Nightmare and Complacency: Razumov and the Western Eye." *Critical Quarterly* IV:197–214 (Autumn 1962).

Van Ghent, Dorothy. "On *Lord Jim*." In her *The English Novel: Form and Function*. New York: Rinehart, 1953.

Warren, Robert Penn. Introduction to *Nostromo*, Modern Library Edition. New York: Random House, 1951. [Reprinted from *Sewanee Review* LIX:363–391 (Summer 1951).] (An important reading that should be compared with Van Ghent's in the present collection.)

Watt, Ian. "Conrad Criticism and *The Nigger of the 'Narcissus*,' " *Nineteenth-Century Fiction* XII:257–283 (March 1958).

————. "Joseph Conrad: Alienation and Commitment." In *The English Mind* Edited by H. S. Davies and George Watson. Cambridge: At the University Press, 1964.

Wiley, Paul. *Conrad's Measure of Man*. Madison: University of Wisconsin Press, 1954.

Young, Vernon. "Joseph Conrad: Outline for a Reconsideration." *Hudson Review* II:5–19 (Spring 1949).

*Zabel, Morton Dauwen. "Conrad." In *Craft and Character in Modern Fiction*. New York: Viking, 1957. (A critic important in the Conrad revival of the 1940s and 1950s.)

Catalog

If you are interested in a list of fine Paperback
books, covering a wide range of subjects
and interests, send your name and address,
requesting your free catalog, to:

McGraw-Hill Paperbacks
1221 Avenue of Americas
New York, N.Y. 10020